Praise for *Walking Tow⌄*

"Walking and hiking, especially in an ancient wilderness, can heal the mind and body. I say this with certainty after my own 3,300 mile walk across America. Read this book as a reminder. Read it as an inspiration. Whether you are trying to manage PTSD or the daily struggles of life, this book is for you. It should be on everyone's shelf."

— Rory Fanning, author, *Worth Fighting For: An Army Ranger's Journey Out of the Military and Across America*

"Cindy Ross has written a book that is an ode to those who serve, an accounting of the true costs of that service, and the stories of healing that only the natural world can bring. Each profile offers courage, hope, and example to all those who have been lost, offering a guide and companion to walking in and with the wilderness to find peace."

— Shannon Huffman Polson, author, *The Grit Factor: Courage, Resilience and Leadership in the Most Male Dominated Organization in the World*

"In *Walking Toward Peace,* Cindy Ross reveals some of the most essential ingredients necessary for veterans healing from the horrors and invisible wounds of war. She shares the stories of two dozen wounded warriors who immerse themselves in nature, giving them compassionate witness and amply demonstrating how nature, storytelling, and community are homecoming elements for *all* warriors. Ross provides these healing examples in a generous and accessible manner."

— Edward Tick, PhD, author, *Warrior's Return: Restoring the Soul After War*

"Cindy Ross's *Walking Toward Peace* is a window into the psychological wounds inflicted on America's combat veterans, as well as a thoughtful consideration of the therapeutic value of long-distance treks in salving those wounds. I found the book to be highly engaging, thought-provoking, and a welcome addition to the literature on the health promoting properties of nature-based recreation."

— Daniel L. Dustin, PhD, author, *Nature's Grace: America's Veterans and the Healing Power of Nature*

"The stories of the veterans and the professional studies Ross cites in *Walking Toward Peace* give a scientific basis to the power of Mother Nature. And, as a person of African American descent, I am happy to see her address veterans of color and the issue of why more are not attracted to the natural world and the need to engage them in outdoor activities."

— Anthony Jackson, Major General, US Marine Corps (Ret) and former Director, California State Parks

"*Walking Toward Peace* provides a rich map to the healing power of long-trail hiking, with waypoints provided by military veterans from Earl Shaffer to men and women coming home today from countless deployments around the world. . . . Readers will realize, however, that the power is in the *journey*, not the destination, and will be impressed by Cindy Ross's adroit writing and trailside intimacy with many of the veterans she meets along the way. I invite you to join in the journey of this book and find some healing of your own."

— Stacy Bare, US Army veteran, adventurer, and filmmaker, *Adventure Not War*

"I am elated by the stories Cindy Ross shares here of how individually and collectively these valiant warriors are able to find solace, peace, and a return to sanity in the comforting arms of our Mother Nature. I hope this book helps enlighten others like me and reinforces the respect and gratitude we owe our defenders and our shared life support-system, Nature."

— Audrey Peterman, author, *Legacy on the Land: A Black Couple Discovers Our National Inheritance and Tells Why Every American Should Care*

"Combining first-hand accounts with compelling and current research, Cindy Ross focuses on the soldiers' capacities and abilities, broadening their personal strength to heal and, over time, improve their mental, spiritual, and physical health. She has provided a beautiful, thoughtful, and useful book that will indeed help veterans but, I would add, also other survivors of trauma."

— Joyce Mikal-Flynn, EdD, FNP, MSN, author, *Anatomy of a Survivor: Building Resilience, Grit, and Growth After Trauma.*

"While many can speak to the restorative aspects of nature, this book magnifies the power of the wild to heal wounds that seem too deep. The intense memories experienced by these veterans are so raw that the pain seems untouchable until they are immersed in the forest, where the adversity of the walk and the healing stillness of nature together offer restoration and wholeness."

— Beth Jones, certified nature forest therapy guide

"*Walking Toward Peace* helps put a face not only on the trauma that war inflicts on our veterans, but also the promise that nature provides them for healing and hope. Cindy Ross helps us to witness examples of this transformation and also understand that nature isn't a miracle cure—but it is a powerful first step in the long journey toward a peaceful soul."

— Teresa Ana Martinez, Executive Director, Continental Divide Trail Coalition

"These stories of warriors finding true solace on the trail show us the resilience of these men and women and how, through connecting with nature and all the pleasure and pain that comes with the physical commitment of a long-distance hike, healing is possible."

— Sandra Marra, President and CEO, Appalachian Trail Conservancy

"Cindy Ross listens, as she hikes with these men and women, to stories that are usually only shared with fellow vets who can truly understand. *Walking Toward Peace* will inspire all those seeking a moment of grace and a path toward healing."

— Kevin Ferris, co-author, *Vets and Pets*

"When we honor our veterans, it is tempting to forget their humanity. Cindy Ross opens a window to the whole stories of men and women deeply affected by war and their time in uniform. She asks the reader to understand that they are not all angels or heroes, but simply individuals who did their duty and want to come home as best they can. Her book offers perhaps the most important tribute we can provide our veterans: the truth."

— Mike Gambone, author, *The Greatest Generation Comes Home: The Veteran in American Society*

"*Walking Toward Peace* places you in the hearts and minds of veterans from different generations and service branches as they struggle with wartime memories. Ross masterfully captures their stories of healing and redemption as they travel the Appalachian Trail and other long-distance routes. This is a must read."

— Brigadier General Jerry Otterbein, US Air Force (Ret)

WALKING

VETERANS HEALING

TOWARD

ON AMERICA'S TRAILS

PEACE

CINDY ROSS

Illustrations by Bryce Ross Gladfelter

MOUNTAINEERS
BOOKS

MOUNTAINEERS BOOKS is dedicated to the exploration, preservation, and enjoyment of outdoor and wilderness areas.

1001 SW Klickitat Way, Suite 201, Seattle, WA 98134
800-553-4453, www.mountaineersbooks.org

Printed in the United States of America
Distributed in the United Kingdom by Cordee, www.cordee.co.uk
24 23 22 21   1 2 3 4 5

Copyeditor: Ellen Wheat
Design and layout: Jen Grable
Cover photograph: iStock/Yarygin
Illustrations: Bryce Ross Gladfelter, www.brycegladfelter.com

Library of Congress Cataloging-in-Publication data is on file for this title at https://lccn.loc.gov/2020045125 (print). The ebook record is https://lccn .loc.gov/2020045126.

Mountaineers Books titles may be purchased for corporate, educational, or other promotional sales, and our authors are available for a wide range of events. For information on special discounts or booking an author, contact our customer service at 800-553-4453 or mbooks@mountaineersbooks.org.

ISBN (paperback): 978-1-68051-303-5
ISBN (ebook): 978-1-68051-304-2

An independent nonprofit publisher since 1960

To the memory of Zachary Adamson and to all the veterans who so courageously opened their hearts and shared their incredibly personal stories of healing.

CONTENTS

All stories have a curious, even dangerous power. They are manifestations of truth—yours and mine. And truth is all at once the most wonderful yet terrifying thing in the world, which makes it nearly impossible to handle. It is such a great responsibility that it's best not to tell a story at all unless you know you can do it right. You must be very careful, or without knowing it, you can change the world.

—Vera Nazarian, *Dreams of the Compass Rose*

PROLOGUE

THE SOFT SOUND OF FALLING rain filled the evening air, pulling our attention to the tattooed man who turned the rainstick. When the hollow cactus tube was flipped, tiny pebbles trickled down the thorns inside, making a rainlike sound, an indication to the group gathered around the campfire that the person then holding the stick had the floor. When the pebbles' sound ceased, all ears and eyes were on the veteran as he told his story.

The Marine spoke of exploding bombs, scraping up Iraqi guts with a shovel, and picking up hands and legs after a suicide bomber drove a dump truck into the soldier's post. He witnessed his best buddies dying. He had been on a dozen different meds to try to cope. "When I came home from the war," he said, "I was still constantly on guard, hypervigilant. I never sat with my back to an entrance or exit. Nightmares jarred me awake in the middle of the night to check and recheck windows and doors whenever I heard a sound." He never slept well and had a hard time finding peace. If snippets of calm did arrive, they didn't last. "It was all so exhausting.... Until I began to walk the Appalachian Trail."

Like our rainstick, a talking stick is a tool used in many Native American cultures when a council is called. It allows all members to speak their sacred point of view, passed from person to person, and only the person holding the stick is allowed to talk. Every member of the meeting must listen closely to the speaker. The Marine shared his symptoms of post-traumatic stress disorder (PTSD), which can result after a terrifying event, such as combat during war or in civilian life after a natural disaster, a serious accident, a terrorist act, a rape, or other violent personal assault. Symptoms of PTSD may include flashbacks, nightmares, and severe anxiety as well as uncontrollable thoughts about the event. Not all veterans suffer from PTSD, and not all are able to talk about their experiences, but in the forest and around the campfire, the group of hiking veterans that we hosted at our Pennsylvania log home felt safe. My husband, Todd Gladfelter, and I might not be members of the military tribe, but we belong to another tightly knit community: long-distance hikers.

The Appalachian Trail is the longest continuously marked footpath in the world, extending from Springer Mountain in Georgia to Mount Katahdin in Maine. When long-distance hikers reach Pennsylvania, the halfway point, they are often at a psychologically low point in their journey. The Tuscarora Sandstone exposed on the ridge of the long, spiny Blue Mountain can trip up even the fittest of hikers. Except for an occasional water gap, the elevation map reads like a cruising trail, and many hikers mistakenly expect to motor through the miles. The heat and humidity soar in July, when thru-hikers typically enter our state, adding to their overall misery. Todd and I knew of this problem intimately. We had each completed the entire 2,180-mile trail and for years managed a hostel along the route near Hawk Mountain Sanctuary in Eckville, Pennsylvania, under the Volunteers-in-Parks (VIP) program of the National Park Service. In 2013 word had spread that a group of veterans was thru-hiking the Appalachian Trail, attempting to heal from their trauma by hiking. I wrote a few pieces on their inspiring endeavor, which were published in various magazines. Todd and I organized a big dinner and gave them a much-needed break from hiking the trail. In return, we hoped they'd share a story or two around the campfire.

SINCE 2001, MORE THAN 2.7 MILLION VETERANS HAVE BEEN TO WAR ZONES in Iraq and Afghanistan. According to a 2019 report on suicide prevention by the US Department of Veterans Affairs, one in five veterans has been diagnosed with PTSD. Many veterans who suffer with PTSD never seek help and have never been diagnosed. An average of seventeen veterans (the number is twenty if you include active duty and National Guard) die by suicide every day, totaling almost sixty thousand veterans since 2010. That is more than the total number of lives lost in more than eighteen years of combat in the Middle East. Our nation has tragically failed these veterans.

These staggering numbers have forced therapists, caregivers, and researchers to find alternatives to traditional therapies and prescribed medications to treat veterans with PTSD, depression, and anxiety. One of the most innovative approaches is ecotherapy, which uses outdoor activities in nature to improve mental and physical well-being. Hundreds of studies conducted in the past decade or so have convinced even the most skeptical that spending time in nature has the power to heal. Since walking is so accessible, hiking is one of the easiest ways to reap the benefits of nature's healing. These veterans at our campfire were hoping to find that along the Appalachian Trail.

OVER THE COURSE OF THE EVENING, MORE VETERANS HELD THE RAINSTICK and shared their stories. It wasn't enough to pack thirty pounds on sore knees and aching muscles; they also hauled war-induced nightmares and memories up the mountains. The trek spurred recollections of years in the service: images of dead comrades, the torment of second-guessing orders, questioning their own survival while others had perished. These thoughts haunted the veterans as they climbed. Mile after mile, though, they began to leave such thoughts behind, to deposit memories on the valley floors and ascend to greater heights of acceptance of their lives and their service. Through hiking, these vets came to terms with much of what they saw, experienced, or may have had to do, just as they accepted nature's harsh terms of steep climbs, rocks and roots, and stormy weather. Their dark pasts began to recede, much as the mountains they summited faded into the distance. They weren't walking *away* from their histories; they were learning to live *with* them and themselves. You cannot get rid of the past, but you can learn to live with it, grow from it, and work to be free from its emotional turmoil.

As they traveled the Appalachian Trail, these veterans experienced a roller coaster of emotions. They shed tears of joy at the beauty of the world and the fate that allowed them to return home while their best friends perished. There were also tears of regret over death and the horror inflicted on fellow human beings. These emotions—survivor guilt, grief, moral injury, shame over killing fellow humans, fury and desolation that others had killed their best friends—fueled their PTSD. As the miles passed, they were able to move, oh so gradually, toward acceptance and forgiveness as they walked toward peace with each step.

These veterans took hold of my heart and inspired me to form the non-profit River House PA, so I could help more veterans. River House often works in tandem with recreational therapists at nearby Veterans Administration health facilities—hosting hikes and paddles as well as campfires and cookouts for the veterans while immersing them in healing nature. In the ensuing years, I have met many inspiring veterans out in nature, working hard to heal and succeeding at it. The heroes profiled throughout this book have shown tremendous courage in opening up and sharing their deeply personal journeys. They have exposed their hearts and souls to fellow veterans and their families to show that there can be light at the end of the dark tunnel, and that light is life. These are their stories.

PART ONE

THE TRAIL PROVIDES

CHAPTER 1

EARL SHAFFER

US ARMY, 1941–1946

Four and a half years of army service, more than half of it in
combat areas of the Pacific, without furlough or even rest leave,
had left me confused and depressed. Perhaps this trip would be
the answer ... [the hike] would be a kill or a cure; it would either
make me worse or make me better.
—Earl Shaffer's journal (1918–2002)

I FINGERED THE SMALL BLACK leather journal in my palm and brought it up to my nose to inhale its scent. More than seventy years old, the journal's soft cover was worn by the fingerprints of a great man, a hero, and a leader. Earl Shaffer, the first person to hike the entire Appalachian Trail in a continuous stretch, carried this journal on his epic journey in 1948, through snow, rain, and baking sun along a huge mountain range. In the archives of the Smithsonian Institution's American History Museum in Washington, DC, I searched through Earl's writings to learn his story as a veteran walking America's iconic trail, attempting to heal. A fellow Pennsylvanian and an Army veteran of World War II, Earl got on the trail to walk off his war. He is the father of long-distance-hiking culture, my pen pal, and a dear friend who directly influenced me as both a writer and a backpacker.

As a communicator in the Army Signal Corps, Earl served in the Pacific Theater and struggled with bouts of depression. According to his biography, *A Grip on the Mane of Life,* written by David Donaldson, Earl once admitted to a Pennsylvania soldier that "if it wasn't against the Bible, I'd commit suicide." In 1947 he returned home from the war feeling hopeless and broken-hearted. He had lost his childhood friend Walter Winemiller in Iwo Jima. Since their adolescence, the two had tramped the Pennsylvania woods until they were both deployed in 1941. They had planned to hike the entire length of the Appalachian Trail when the war was over. For two years Earl wandered about feeling unsettled. Attending college on the GI Bill was not an option Earl entertained because, as he wrote, "he feared it would force him into the same mold as everyone else."

About that time, Earl read in a magazine that the Appalachian Trail had suffered serious neglect since he and Walt had first sprouted their dream. During the war, maintenance had ceased, and many considered an end-to-end hike impossible. No one had ever thru-hiked the trail, and now it was in real danger of disappearing. Earl saw it as a personal challenge. "I'll do it to get over the Army," he later wrote about the decision. "I'll take pictures and keep a notebook so I could write a book about it." He hoped his hike would generate publicity and rekindle interest in restoring the entire Appalachian Trail. He set off alone, bringing Walt along in his memory.

AFTER WORLD WAR II, SUFFERING VETERANS WERE TREATED A LITTLE better than their World War I counterparts. Some veterans in that earlier generation experienced truly grisly responses to their trauma: shot by their own for cowardice or enduring electric shocks applied to their necks, cigarettes put out on their tongues, or hot plates pressed at the back of the throat to make them snap out of their distress.

The suffering of World War II veterans was better understood by doctors as a mental disorder they called "shell shock." Passed in 1946 and signed into law by President Harry Truman, the National Mental Health Act included the creation of VA medical centers that treated mental health problems associated with war and were the start of psychological counseling for veterans. Electric shock was then considered the best available psychiatric therapy for treating depression and disturbed behaviors. Antipsychotic or antidepressant medications did not yet exist, nor was there advanced technology like MRIs (magnetic resonance imaging) or super-microscopes that help doctors understand and evaluate psychological and physical trauma to the human brain.

Over the years the term "shell shock" was replaced with "combat stress reaction" (CSR), also known as "battle fatigue." But it wasn't until 1980 that the American Psychiatric Association's third edition of the *Diagnostic and Statistical Manual of Mental Disorders* named the mental condition as post-traumatic stress disorder (PTSD). This new diagnosis came about because the field of psychology and psychotherapy had grown and new research had occurred. After the Vietnam War and the enormous num-bers of veterans returning with PTSD, fresh research and the use of new technology in treatment improved our understanding of the human brain and how it reacts to and changes as a result of trauma.

Although many advances have been made in the past few decades, PTSD continues to carry a weighty stigma for today's veterans. Back in Earl Shaffer's time, few veterans sought help for their condition. Instead, Earl attempted to walk off the war along the length of the Appalachian Trail. His plan was to move north with the spring, "with no definite day by day goals but never tarrying long, as weather and terrain permitted." He hoped an early start from the south would give him at least six months to reach "the timberline of New England." As he wrote in his journal: "And now the time had come. Why not walk the army out of my system, both mentally and physically, take pictures and notes along the way, make a regular expedition out of it. It will benefit me at a time of very low ebb."

THE APPALACHIAN TRAIL WAS THE DREAM OF FORESTER BENTON MACKAYE, who also conceived the idea of the Interstate Highway system in the 1940s and collaborated with Gifford Pinchot, the first chief of the US Forest Ser-vice, to establish the country's system of national forests and parks. The trail was completed and designated by the Appalachian Trail Conference (ATC) in 1937 (renamed the Appalachian Trail Conservancy in 2005) after twenty-five years of planning and construction. Today, the ATC is a con-federation of many local hiking clubs that organize thousands of volun-teers to build and maintain the trail as well as 225 three-sided log shelters positioned approximately a day's walk apart. Shelters offer protection from weather and are usually located near springs to provide drinking water for the night. The war effort had taken away the trail maintainers, and while servicemen wreaked havoc on US enemies overseas, the green briar and the blowdowns wreaked havoc on the Appalachian Trail.

Armed with compass, roadmap, a pith helmet, and his army gear, Earl began the trail in Georgia and headed north, often walking sockless in his army boots. He searched for the two-by-six-inch white blazes painted on the trees that pointed north. According to his journal, Earl spent much of his journey searching for the trail, sometimes looking for signs that it even existed. He wrote about these challenges, and between the lines there was evidence of how nature seemed to be healing him.

Earl described his first night in North Carolina's Smoky Mountains: "I fell asleep to the lullaby of the wind in the trees and the somewhere calling of a whip-poor-will." He wrote about the countless chance meetings with locals who administered "trail magic"—feeding him, giving him a bed for the night, and providing much-needed conversation and company. These encounters fed Earl's soul. When he stepped into a dark old-growth forest to make his camp for the night, he "heard for the second time in [his] life the awesome sound of a giant tree falling somewhere in the stillness." When he found his way at night to Speck Pond in Maine and the comfort of a shelter by following the sound of the singing tree frogs, he wrote: "Ever since, when the homeland meadows are turning green and the silvery lilt of those tiny peepers livens the night, I think of the time when they helped me 'come to port' on the Long Cruise."

In addition to experiencing some aspects of healing through the kind and helpful strangers he encountered, he felt safe enough to enjoy beautiful things: a presence of the Divine in old-growth forests, the skies, and a healthy rhythm from the daily and seasonal cycles. Despite the challenges of an unmarked and unmaintained trail, weather extremes, and physical hardships, hiking on the Appalachian Trail was right where Earl wanted to be. He was coming to port, walking back to peace, to himself. In his journal he never mentioned what occurred in the war; rather, he focused on the present moment, working on the task at hand, walking to Maine, his war memories fading into the past.

Decades before "mindfulness" became a buzzword used by mainstream therapists, Earl was intuitively a practitioner of this form of therapy. The state of having an open, expansive awareness and living in the present was associated with Buddhists at the turn of the nineteenth century. These religious men sought a heightened state of consciousness, but Earl was mindful out of necessity. On the trail he needed to stay acutely aware of his surroundings, as well as what lay at his feet, to find his way. He realized he could not expect to reach Maine if he hiked mindlessly.

THE PAGES OF EARL'S LEATHER JOURNAL ARE COVERED WITH EXPRESSIVE cursive handwriting, scribed with a fountain pen that bled through some of the pages, probably when the night was damp. In the back of the journal are Earl's poems—he was a poet as well as a long-distance backpacker. His feelings, his grief about the war, his joy and love of the natural world pour forth through his poetry. It is possible to follow his thoughts while he was composing, since he crossed out words in search of better ones to describe his feelings. Reading these poems, you can almost smell his musty tent and the wetness of the Appalachian woods, as he likely set down his words by candlelight.

> *Go ye out to the mountains*
> *Far far from a town*
> *Stretch yourself on the clean forest floor*
> *Gaze aloft through the canopy*
> *To frown and remember your troubles no more*

The Smithsonian archives contain a cover letter Earl wrote to Doubleday Books introducing his poems for possible publication. He did not think of having the story of his Appalachian Trail journey published at that time, but he had hopes for his poems, which he described to the publisher in detail:

> Many of these verses were written under the most difficult conditions, often by firelight, flashlight, candlelight or moonlight, and

sometimes key phrases were scribbled blindly during total black-out. I carried the ever-growing collection with me all over the Pacific, in and out of customs, on shipboard, in planes, hunched in mosquito bars, on mail sacks, in pup tents. The results are not calculated to be sophisticated but rather are meant to record a portion of the intricate pattern of global conflict, as seen by a soldier who was a minute part of it.

Through poetry, it seems, Earl processed the emotions and the experiences he had endured in combat. He grieved the situations, experienced the anger, the horror, the sadness, and the guilt, rather than remaining stuck in avoiding uncomfortable emotions. "My purpose in writing," he further explained in the letter to Doubleday, "is to help provide some understanding of what I and my buddies experienced, in the hope that such knowledge will be of value in shaping a better future." Unfortunately, his poems are not included in the Smithsonian collection. The archive historian I spoke with had no idea what had become of them. However, his Appalachian Trail memoir, *Walking with Spring,* was eventually published by the Appalachian Trail Conference in 1982.

Even though Earl and I had been pen pals for more than a dozen years, I didn't meet him in person until 1995, when he was seventy-five years old. He looked closer to fifty—strong, well-built, glowing from a life of living healthy—and he had maintained the same weight for fifty-five years, never needed a doctor, and took no medications. At his home in rural York County, Pennsylvania, Earl raised chickens and goats, kept bees, grew his own organic food, and maintained an orchard. A hand-dug, spring-fed pond was his water source, and a hand-laid-stone road through a swampy field led to his property. Living a simple lifestyle close to the earth and working the soil with his hands, Earl found a therapeutic way to live.

Earl innately realized it back then, although research had not yet discovered that an antidepressant microbe, *Mycobacterium vaccae,* that lives in soil boosts happiness levels in humans. The microbe mirrors the effect that mind-altering drugs like Prozac have on neurons in the brain, causing levels of cytokines (cell-signaling molecules) to rise. Gardeners manipulate the soil, which releases the bacterium they touch and inhale. The cytokines stimulate the release of serotonin and norepinephrine, two neurotransmitting chemicals that make people relaxed and happy. The druglike effects of this soil bacterium were accidently discovered in 2004 by Mary O'Brien, an oncologist at the Royal Marsden Hospital in London. She created a serum from the microbe in hopes of boosting the immune system of lung cancer patients. Instead, it boosted their moods.

Neuroscientist Christopher Lowry at the University of Colorado Boulder, along with Lisa Brenner, the director of the Veterans Affairs Rocky Mountain Mental Illness Research, Education, and Clinical Center in Denver, are conducting research using *Mycobacterium vaccae* with veterans suffering from PTSD and mild traumatic brain injury. Today, national nonprofit programs such as Warriors That Farm, Veteran Farmer Coalition, and Veterans to Farmers help vets heal through farming, gardening, and beekeeping. Earl was onto something, but the science was still a mystery at the time.

Besides growing much of his own food, Earl earned a great deal of his income from peddling goods at flea markets, a livelihood that paralleled his beliefs in recycling and reusing. In his youth, he paid for his clothes with money made from trapping furs, often with his friend Walter, and selling his handiwork. The freedom he found walking off the war from Georgia to Maine became such a need that he devised ways to support himself and weave that freedom into his everyday life.

Earl and I had a lot in common. After I completed my thru-hike of the Appalachian Trail in 1979, we wrote long, handwritten letters to each other. Hiking the trail had coaxed the writer out of me, and as it had been for Earl, the trail was a great source of inspiration. I shared the manuscript of my first book, *A Woman's Journey on the Appalachian Trail*, with him, and he offered generous feedback. Handwritten in calligraphy and illustrated with 125 ink-and-charcoal drawings, that book was published in 1982, the same year as Earl's *Walking with Spring*, and both are still in print.

The Appalachian Trail Conservancy's publisher, Brian King, told me that for years Earl would stop in at ATC's headquarters whenever he was in the area. The two men would sit and chat, and Earl would still tear up, decades later, when he spoke about the loss of his friend Walter. Perhaps what was most therapeutic for Earl after hiking the trail was how he designed his life. He had realized that finding a sense of purpose larger than himself was critical for healing. It is especially important for those who suffer with depression, which often accompanies PTSD, along with low self-esteem, finding little to no pleasure in anything, and holding at best a dim sense of hope for the future.

After his journey on the Appalachian Trail, Earl went on to build, maintain, and relocate the trail; construct shelters; organize trail clubs; and share advice with new and fellow hikers. Hiking the trail gave Earl his life back, and in turn he devoted his life to the trail. In 1965, feeling "restless and at loose ends," Earl successfully hiked the entire Appalachian Trail a second time. And at the age of seventy-nine, on the fiftieth anniversary of his first thru-hike, he hiked it a third time. A lot of trail magic was extended to him on that third hike, for Earl had since turned into a trail hero. Earl died five years later, after a lifetime of paving the way for long-distance hikers, many of whom are veterans.

THE DESK ON WHICH I WROTE THIS BOOK WAS A GIFT FROM EARL. IT SITS in the hand-hewn log cabin that my husband, Todd, built for me. During a visit to Earl's home, Todd and I were invited to explore his barn of refinished antiques and found a perfect American chestnut table with thick turned legs that he had stripped of paint. Countless times, I've slid my hands over the table's smooth wooden surface, knowing that Earl's hands rubbed oil into its grain. Since Earl thru-hiked the Appalachian Trail in 1948, more than twenty thousand hikers have completed the same journey. He helped to create a whole culture of people, including America's veterans, who go to our trails seeking health, rejuvenation, and peace on their own terms. The trail provides.

CHAPTER 2

STEVE CLENDENNING

US MARINE CORPS, 1992–2013

*If you bring forth what is inside you, what you bring forth will
save you. If you don't bring forth what is inside you, what you
bring forth can destroy you.*
—*Gospel of Thomas,* 70

WITH RAINSTICK IN HAND, STEVE Clendenning slumped low in his chair
by the campfire. He had just shared some effects his wartime memories had
on his body and his soul. Taking a break before continuing, he rocked gently
as if to shake his words free. Surrounded by the Pennsylvania woods and a
few other hikers, Steve stroked his blond beard over and over with his left
hand. His southern drawl broke as he shared his story of war in Iraq.

"We were doing a road sweep in Fallujah," Steve began, "covering the
street with a mine detector. It was pitch black out and we were wearing
night goggles. That particular road was a mess with mines. It even got the
nickname, IED Alley." The first team leader and the engineer spotted a hole
in the road where an IED had blown up the night before. The hole had not
been filled in, so the team climbed in to check it out. "All of a sudden it
blew," he recalled. When Steve turned on the Humvee's white lights, he
saw flesh and blood at his feet. A Marine ran toward him with a devastating
report: "Staff Sergeant, I found him and it's just his torso." Steve approached

and said a prayer to God for the deceased. "I walked another one hundred meters down the road and found his leg and more pieces. We scraped up his remains and put his body parts in the back of the truck. He was my buddy."

Raising his lowered eyes from the flickering fire, Steve stared outward before picking up the thread. "The next morning my truck got blown to shit by an IED," he said. "After we opened fire and chased down the insurgents, we went to the hospital. I had traumatic brain injury and my hearing was severely damaged. I never felt normal again."

He asked himself, "How can you walk up to your friend and find him like that and not have it profoundly impact you for the rest of your life? How could you come back from that?" With his blue eyes shaded by a brimmed camouflage hat, his boyish face revealed the answer: you don't. Like World War II veteran Earl Shaffer had before him, Steve was walking off his war as he hiked the length of the Appalachian Trail, to rid the demons from his head, to heal from his PTSD. This was a different kind of mission.

NEXT TO STEVE THAT EVENING AROUND THE CAMPFIRE SAT HIS WIFE, RUBY Clendenning, a striking long-haired woman of Mexican descent. Her arm embraced her husband's shoulders. A Marine herself, Ruby also suffered from PTSD, a result of sexual assault in the military. Although the cause of the trauma was different, Ruby understood her husband's pain.

"Back then, I could not go into public places," Steve said. "I was on too many medications and behaved like a zombie. I was in a complete funk, would not shower, or eat." On the one-year anniversary of the exploding-IED injury and losing his friend, Steve tried to take his own life. "I got drunk out of my mind. I moved the car out of the garage, opened up the ladder to the attic door, and fashioned an extension cord into a noose which I hung from the rafters." He doesn't know how he did it—he had never tied a noose before. He stood on the ladder with his phone in his hand, texting everyone he loved. "I could not stand the images in my brain anymore, or the night-mares, and I wanted them to go away." At the exact right moment, Ruby walked into the garage and found Steve. She had woken in the middle of the night, rolled over in bed, and noticed he was gone. She had searched the house for him, fortunately finding him in time..

Steve was put into a psychiatrist's care. He spent four years at the Marine Corps Wounded Warrior Battalion located at Camp Lejeune in North Carolina. After retiring from the military, he's been going to doctors, attending weekly counseling, and having brain scans. He gained weight and had a hard time finding peace. Then he learned about the Appalachian Trail, Earl Shaffer's therapeutic hike in 1948, and the path's potential for healing trauma. He loaded up a backpack and headed for the southern end of the AT in Georgia.

STEVE SET OUT WITH A GROUP OF HIKERS AND, AS THE DAYS AND MILES ticked by, the journey indeed brought him a sense of peace. The hike was not without major challenges, however. There was a norovirus outbreak in Virginia, and along the trail Steve became so sick that he was hospitalized and had to have his appendix removed. After a five-day hospital stay and another eight days of recovery at home, Steve resumed his hike. During those two weeks off the trail to recuperate, he began to fall apart mentally and felt his PTSD returning in full force. "All I had to do was open up the oven door when the stove was on, and I was right back in Iraq," Steve remembered. "That oppressive heat flooding out reminded me of exiting the air-conditioned Humvee and the Iraqi heat slamming me." His response to the open oven door is an example of what is known as "body memory," when a sensory experience triggers a traumatic memory.

Steve missed his fellow hikers, the trail, and the peace that the journey had brought him. Off-trail, his nightmares returned as well as his anger. One time when Steve and Ruby were shopping at the local Walmart for trail food and supplies, his rage got the best of him. In the first-aid aisle, a teenager in a hoodie zoomed by in a motorized wheelchair, almost clipping Steve and Ruby. Steve stopped him and said, "What are you doing? Those are for people who need them."

The boy said he'd hurt his ankle and sped away. A minute later, a girl flew by. "Get off that and leave it right here," Steve called after the kid, but she ignored him. Then Steve saw the pair walking in the next aisle. Incensed, he yelled, "Hey! You're walking just fine now. Your ankle must not be hurt anymore."

"Uh, yeah, it feels a little better," the teenager said. But Steve was not having it. "You're full of shit," he said. It was the girl's response that really escalated things for Steve. "Oh you must be real badass that you're picking on little kids," she said.

"He don't look like no little kid to me," said Steve, as he moved a little closer.

Ruby anticipated trouble and ran off to get the manager. When he arrived on the scene, Steve let him have it. "You'd better get these kids out of here, or I'm gonna put blood all over the front of your building. You don't know who you're dealing with here! You have no idea what shit I have been through!" The manager promptly escorted the kids out of the store, but in a few minutes the boy returned and took a photo of Steve with his cell phone. Steve threw everything he was holding onto the floor and went after the boy. Ruby tried to grab him and hold him back, but couldn't. The manager chased Steve outside.

In the parking lot, Steve finally calmed down. "It could have been real bad," Ruby said. "If Steve would have put his hands on those kids, he would have gotten himself in trouble. When something trips his temper, he can't control it."

Steve explained his behavior this way: "Anger is what comes out when all the other emotions from the war build up. It's survivor's guilt. Why am I here and why didn't those other guys make it?" Anger is sadness coming out sideways. Explosive anger is a reaction cultivated in the military to survive in combat. But this approach doesn't work in normal society.

STEVE DID NOT WANT TO BE ANGRY ANYMORE, AND HE FOUND THAT ECO-therapy provided a path to letting go. As clinical psychologist Lynne Williams explains: "Being in nature, whether a walk in a leafy park, a paddle on a lake, or a longer hiking trip, all help shift the brain to the relaxed, calm, focused electrical brainwave pattern. Our brains run on electricity, with various wave patterns being involved in various experiences and activities. Learning to switch to the relaxed alpha pattern (through nature, creativity, interacting with pets, water sounds, classical music, to name some activities) helps rewire the emotionally dysregulated PTSD brain into a calmer, focused one capable of new learning and new experiences."

Ruby encouraged Steve's hiking the Appalachian Trail. She told him he should not quit regardless of how many times he was in the hospital, sick, or injured. He had to go back and finish what he started, although his absence was hard on Ruby. "It's a sacrifice for us left behind too. I'm not home making fuckin' cupcakes." She worked full-time as a Marine at Camp Lejeune's Department of Defense while also running the household and emotionally supporting her husband on the trail (they spoke frequently by phone). She visited Steve twice on the trail as he traveled northward. Every time she saw him, she initially thought: I have my old Steve back. "But then he would say or do something, and I'd know he wasn't a hundred percent."

Ruby didn't question the sacrifice. "Steve is my best friend. I don't ever question the money he spent or the time he has been away. I can't put a dollar price on getting my husband back. I just want the Steve back that I married. And if I can't, I want him as good as I can get." A few months later, with a thousand more miles on the soles of his boots, Steve reached Mount Katahdin in Maine, the end of the Appalachian Trail. The long journey had provided indeed, helping Steve walk his way out of anger, toward a place of peace.

> I was a big tough Marine a few years back. I killed a lot of people. I "hunted humans." The military takes some things away from you, in order to enable you to kill your fellow man and keep yourself alive. But once you return to normal life, those are the same things that you need in order to function. I've always been a sensitive guy, and after I became wounded and gathered up what remained of my best friend in Iraq, I became even more sensitive and then I broke. I cry when I'm moved. I scream like a little kid when I get scared or surprised. I have a lot of Marine friends who are still acting tough and playing the hard, mean act, and drinking heavily. For me, I'm on the long road back to myself, and the Appalachian Trail helped me find my way.
>
> Don't be mistaken, I may not have walked every mile and every blaze, but what I did this summer will forever live with me as the most adventurous, most breathtaking, and by far the most emotional thing I've ever done. I've been happy and I've laughed so hard I peed myself. I've been sad and I've cried some pretty

emotional tears. I've been so mad over war memories that I could have uprooted trees. I've been miserable from frozen shoes and water bottles, but was amazed that in single-digit temps I still managed to sweat like I was on patrol with 120 pounds of gear in 120-degree temps. I've lost an organ on this trail, and I still came back to see what else the trail had to offer. I've been lonely at times and been full of every emotion you can think of in the last six months, and not just anger! I've made friends on the trail that will forever remain my family for as long as God chooses to leave me here.

My walk sure didn't cure things in six months, but it gave me even more appreciation for life—kind of like what I felt when I realized I was still alive after being hit in Fallujah. I may never be the same person I was before Iraq, but Mother Nature sure did give me a place to "take it easy" and smell the roses.

Way back in 1992, I went to Marine Corps boot camp and was told I stood ten feet tall and was bulletproof and could outrun a roadrunner. I lost that feeling a few years ago, but I can now say that feeling has returned. I can climb any mountain, ford any stream, build a fire with wet wood, and eat things that could make a billy goat puke. I feel as if I'm still on Mount Katahdin looking down saying, "Wow! Look what I did!" Feels pretty amazing. And just like earning the title and honor of being a United States Marine, you can't take that away from me . . . ever. The trail provides.

The summer of 2013 will forever be the greatest and most grueling time of my life. I might have hurt all day long from hiking up a mountain, but when I got to a lookout and could see forever and reflect on what God has created and the people in my life that I have lost—I realized that I really needed this hike. I'm going to live my life for those that couldn't.

CHAPTER 3

ADAM BAUTZ

US MARINE CORPS, 2004–2008

TRUDGING UP THE RED SANDSTONE slopes in the Nevada desert, I kept my eyes on the "AT" symbol tattooed on my guide's right calf. Surrounding the symbol was the motto "It's not about the miles, it's about the smiles." Adam Bautz's left calf has a tattoo of a Marine walking away with a machine gun on his shoulders. The last time I'd seen him, he was thru-hiking the Appalachian Trail in Pennsylvania with fellow Marine Tommy Gathman. His blank right calf had yet to earn its AT stamp. Although he cannot easily see the tats himself, their very presence helps Adam provoke conversation with his hiking clients and establish connections.

Here in the Valley of Fire northeast of Las Vegas, Adam is home. He knows it intimately, all forty-six thousand acres of it. He taught himself the area's natural history and can share all kinds of interesting facts about the wildflowers and animals with his hiking comrades. Since 2017, Outdoor Travel Tours, Adam's tour company, has led folks into the desert so they can fall in love with it too. "This is the most amazing place I have ever seen in my life," he said. "It consumes me. There are arches, natural holes, and petroglyphs, and all are easily accessible. There are lizards, flowering cacti, and Gila monsters. Four thousand years ago, Native Americans roamed this very land."

As we hiked into the dazzling Nevada desert, Adam recited the Marine machine gunner description, which he had memorized and recited countless times in his head while deployed to Iraq: "A machine gunner is to provide a heavy volume of close, continuous, accurate support of fire to suppress and destroy all enemy personnel out of small arm's capability." Adam had carried this knowledge on a card in his shirt pocket along with a notebook that contained everything he needed to know as a machine gunner. He could disassemble and reassemble his machine gun in three minutes. He took his job seriously.

Toward the end of Adam's first deployment, an IED blew up a truck carrying three of his comrades, one of whom was a fellow machine gunner. "Why not me?" Adam wondered. "It so easily could have been me." There was little time to grieve, and they had to continue going out on the next patrol. "We would come back from a patrol and there would be empty beds." Adam constantly thought he would be next, incessantly fearing his own death. "Imagine going out every day, knowing people are trying to kill you," he said. "That's a horrible fucking feeling, just waiting to possibly blow up and die."

When Adam got out of the military, certain noises and smells brought him back to the war. "I fell into a deep hole and became a fat bastard. Pair that self-image with my PTSD and it was really hard." To cope, his mind would return to his boyhood stomping grounds on his grandfather's six-hundred-acre wilderness property in Maine. There he had enjoyed his favorite activities of hunting, kayaking, mountain biking, and hiking. He remembered what his grandfather taught him: there is peace and hope in the natural world.

ADAM EVENTUALLY MOVED TO LAS VEGAS AND LANDED A JOB DRIVING AN armored truck for Brink's security. In a single casino stop, he picked up $14 million, mostly money that people had lost. It was then that he realized he did not have to sacrifice happiness for a paycheck, so at his father's suggestion, he became a desert guide for a tour company. One of the companies he worked for was Bullets and Burgers, an outfit for which he guided novices into the desert where they got to shoot machine guns. Then Adam got a phone call from a Marine brother, Tom Gathman.

In Iraq, Adam's machine gun squad had been attached to Tom's rifleman squad, part of the First Platoon. They had lived in the same bunkroom for seven months and quickly became friends. When Tom called to ask Adam if he wanted to quit his job as a tour guide and join him on an Appalachian Trail thru-hike the next year, Adam said, "Hell, yes." Adam knew he wanted to travel, to experience freedom again. "As a Marine, we fought for freedom," he said, "but I did not have it and I wanted it."

Prior to joining the Marines, both men had a tendency to get into trouble with the law and both had pending misdemeanor charges. Enlisting in the Marines, however, cleared their records and put them on a more sustainable path. In that sense, the Corps saved their lives. "I didn't enlist in the Marines for the country," Adam said. "I needed direction and discipline in my life. The majority of us were kids who didn't know what we were signing up for at the time. My mission was to stay alive and keep the others next to me alive." There are many reasons to join the military but, perhaps surprisingly, service to your country is not always number one. According to exhaustive surveys conducted by the global-policy think tank, the RAND Corporation, which offers research and analysis to the US Armed Forces, the overwhelming majority of servicemen and servicewomen cite economic reasons for enlisting. Military service seems to be a job first and a calling second. Some are attracted to benefits like the GI Bill, and others—like Adam and Tommy—are seeking direction in their lives or merely want to get out of Dodge.

I MET ADAM AND TOMMY THE WINTER BEFORE THEY BEGAN THEIR THRU-hike. Tom hails from a small town in Pennsylvania, not far from my home, so I invited the men down for dinner to discuss any last-minute trail-related questions they might have and for an overnight stay in the cabin on our property. When I learned it was Tom's birthday, I baked him a cake, lit candles, and sang. That evening started our wonderful friendship.

When Adam and Tom hiked past my home on the Appalachian Trail, two-and-a-half months after our evening together and a little over a thousand miles into their long hike, I offered them some trail magic—showers, meals, and some "slack-packing"—the term for when a thru-hiker gets to day hike a stretch without the burden of overnight gear and supplies. (With our children grown and out of the nest, Todd and I enjoy helping hikers). I kept their gear and returned them the next morning to the same road

crossing where I had picked them up the evening before. I slack-packed
them for four days and got to hear more of their stories.

Tom called Adam by his trail name, "Machine." There were two reasons for the name: he was a machine gunner, and he hiked like a machine.
Adam could hike seventeen-mile days in Georgia when most thru-hikers
struggled to do ten. "Tom was the only one who could push himself like
me," explained Adam, "and I like to think I was the only one, back then, who
could push him to greater heights." The two men had a lot of fun competing
with each other and took turns leading and setting the pace. "Whoever had
farts that day was in the rear," Adam clarified.

Adam did a lot of thinking on the trail. He relived scenes from Iraq, but
with each mile he was processing his emotions, doing the thinking necessary to grieve, heal, and grow. Gradually, he replaced those scenes with
new thoughts about how to move forward and live better. "I was exposed to
fucked-up shit before the military and also in the military," he said. "I didn't
want to continue living like that." While in the military, Adam participated
in a study on post-traumatic stress. "This shit isn't going to go away," he
realized. Losing brothers, with no opportunity to grieve but moving on to
continue with the mission; getting rocket-propelled grenades (RPGs) shot
at him, and picking up body parts—it all took its toll.

The VA wanted to prescribe a cocktail of meds for Adam, but he never
took them. His troubled childhood showed him what abusing prescription pills looked like, and he wanted nothing to do with drugs. He had even
refused prescribed Vicodin in 2009 after a motorcycle accident required
seventy stitches. Adam had tried talk therapy before the thru-hike, but it
had not been a productive experience. His therapist had been a chaplain in
the Middle East, and when Adam shared how he had prayed over dead bodies, the chaplain began to cry. "I felt like the therapist," he said. "I thought,
'fuck this shit' and I left there with more post-traumatic stress than when
I came in."

ALTHOUGH ADAM HAD FOND ASSOCIATIONS WITH NATURE FROM HIS
grandfather, he never felt its true power until he was on the Appalachian
Trail. On the journey, he finally began to trust people again. He met strangers along the way and started to feel that he wanted to embrace them. "Once

you have seen evil in the world, you assume it is everywhere," he explained. "But I came to realize that I fought for these people. So many things changed on the trail. I also fell in love with Nicole."

One week before leaving for the hike, Adam met Nicole and fell in love at first sight. For more than a thousand miles, the couple stayed in close contact and talked nearly every day. As a surprise, I arranged for Nicole to be at my house in Pennsylvania when Adam passed through on the trail. "At first, it was really hard for me to deal with Adam not showing any emotion," Nicole recalled. "For so long he had suppressed them. He saw many terrible things. He didn't talk openly about his feelings before, but his time on the trail really helped him open up." The trail had provided some clarity, peace.

"I was a whole different species," Adam said. "I never wanted to settle down before Nicole, but as soon as we met, we were so immediately sure of each other." After fifteen hundred miles, he decided to get off the trail and begin his life with Nicole. "You are out here to benefit you, to find peace in nature. If it becomes more stressful to stay, then it's your time to go. I celebrated that I got as far as I did on the trail. The AT showed me how to long-distance hike. It showed me that I can go back out there, again and again, and I will return to the AT in my life." It was a very hard decision, but the trail had worked its magic on Adam.

The couple planned an epic nine-month trip. They sold their belongings and their vehicles, found homes for their dogs, and headed to New Zealand. "As far as walking goes," Adam said, "if anyone gifts themselves a long period of time to walk, and allows their mind to let go, they will realize that thinking is not a bad thing. Out here, you are finally able to think. You go into the Marines and throw your hat in the air when you graduate, but when you get out, you are absolutely lost. You don't know what to do, and if you take the wrong road you're fucked. You learn out here to accept, not forget what happened in the military." After all, acceptance is the final stage in the grieving process.

AFTER NICOLE AND ADAM'S AROUND-THE-WORLD TRIP, THE COUPLE MARried and settled in Las Vegas, and he started his own guide business. Like Nicole, Nevada had captured Adam's heart. Since his AT hike, he has a different way of going about things. Instead of pretending his trauma is not there, Adam has learned to accommodate it and cope. He still has his moments and nightmares, but he handles them a lot better. And Nicole helps. "She grounds me," Adam says. "Without my foundation, I could never stand up." He isn't trying to get back to who he was. He doesn't want to be that type of high-anxiety person anymore. He is much calmer and has that same effect on others.

Adam is working on accepting that his PTSD won't disappear, but he can manage the symptoms when they show up. "Now I go with the happiest choice," he says. "I go with the outcome of fun. I decided that I will always choose the path that creates joy. I aim to never get disgruntled. I laugh at flat tires. I can stay optimistic when it gets really shitty. I know it will come out better. I have no regrets in my life. If it wasn't for all those hardships I experienced, as well as being a Marine and serving my country, I would not be the man I am today."

On the AT, Adam learned to make conversation with strangers. Having thru-hiked the AT and lived on the trail gives him credibility in the eyes of his tour customers. As a guide, he goes a few steps farther than most. He takes a lot of photos of his clients, and within hours they have a direct link to their photo album. He has guided folks from the Netherlands, Germany, Israel, and Tasmania, all within the first year of his business.

> People might get scared out here in the desert on our hikes, but they experience a breakthrough when they leave their comfort zone. I go out of my way to encourage them. I show them how to lock hands and help one another over an obstacle. It is extremely gratifying to help people realize what they are made of. I get that amazing honor by revealing how hiking has benefitted me and is everything in my life. Some of these people have never seen the screen on their phone say 'no service' except in an airplane, but it is wilderness out here. Some have never been on a hike before. It isn't all butterflies and rainbows, but it is hard to get an awkward moment out of me. I won't let it happen.

ADAM LED ME ON TWO EARLY-MORNING HIKES BEFORE THE SUN CLIMBED high in the desert sky and grew hot. We went to one of his favorite spots, called "Fire Wave." We saw an amazing array of flowering cacti and watched lizards emerge from rocks and pose for their portraits. Adam offered me his hand when we traversed a ledge and gave me a boost when we took a long step. On the way back to his vehicle, as I watched his calf muscle flex and move his AT tattoo, I was reminded of his start in nature and all he has overcome and accomplished since then. He has learned to notice beauty, he has learned new things that are not related to survival, and how to share them with others—all aspects of peacetime living.

Adam has come a long way, thanks to the healing power of his time on the trail. Leading researcher Simone Kühn of the Max Planck Institute for Human Development in Berlin explains it this way: "Living in the vicinity of nature has a profound and far-reaching impact on longevity, levels of aggression, cognitive development, and even how kind we are to others." Adam has some advice for veterans: "Try to go as natural as possible with your healing and remedies. Find something that you truly love to do and do it." He is more comfortable out in the desert than he is at home within four walls. "Hiking is my outlet. I like the physical part, the exploration of it. Hiking encourages you to be in the moment, to focus." And the science of being in nature bears this out, as psychologist Lynne Williams explains: "Natural daylight also helps with depression, keeping circadian rhythms appropriate. Exercise reduces stress, produces our body's natural form of morphine (which helps with physical and emotional pain), and produces serotonin, an important hormone and neurotransmitter for good mental health." Being in nature cues up relaxed, calm, focused alpha waves in the brain.

"My worst days are when I don't get outdoors," Adam says. "Nature is my therapy. It is my fitness, my livelihood. It is everything to me." After a guided hike, when clients ask how many miles they hiked on the way back to their car, Adam replies with a satisfied grin, "It's not about the miles, it's about the smiles."

CHAPTER 4

TOM GATHMAN

US MARINE CORPS, 2006–2010

THE FIRST THING THAT STRIKES you when meeting Marine veteran Tom Gathman is his happy-go-lucky nature. His goofball antics, infectious sense of humor, and frequent laughter are not typical personality traits of a combat veteran. How can this Marine, who served two tours in Iraq, during the most intense time of the war, appear so unscathed? His first deployment was in 2007. On foot patrol at a security post, he was run ragged doing intense, exhausting, grueling work. On his second tour (with his buddy Adam Bautz, profiled in the preceding chapter) Tom performed clandestine operations in a surveillance and target-acquisition platoon. He saw some horrible shit in Iraq and did some things he isn't proud of, but he appears to have figured out the way to happiness. In a roundabout way, the Marines led Tom to the trail and the life it provides.

In high school Tom was on a path of self-destruction. As young as thirteen, he began running with a bad crowd; in fact he was the ringleader. At eighteen, he took his father's car to a local university frat party, and after a full day of consuming alcohol, he laid on the gas pedal and ran the car through the state representative's garage. Subsequently tried as an adult, he was put on probation for "driving under the influence." While on probation, Tom did not pay his fines and continued to drive despite his suspended license. After three years of this downward spiral, his actions reached a boiling point. At twenty-two, Tom was sentenced to forty-three days in jail.

Sitting in jail, Tom thought about the direction his life had taken. "How did it come to this?" he wondered. Could he change? He had a good family, but his parents could not help him; he had pushed them away. He was in a revolving-door system. "I needed to get out of it *now!*" Tom approached his probation officer and the judge, asking, "Can I do this another way, so there is a light at the end of the tunnel? Can I join the Marines?" To his surprise, they agreed: "If you prove that you will give your ass to the military, and graduate, we'll squash your record. You'll be a free man." As Tom tells it, "I needed to do something I could be proud of; something to give me discipline and a good life. My parents tried everything on me. The same things that worked for my siblings did not work for me. They were very loving parents. They always wanted the best for me. I don't know how they did it. I put my mother through a depression. She had three good apples and one bad one." Six months after his release, Tom was on a bus to Parris Island, South Carolina, where he attended the Marine Corps School of Infantry, graduated with honors, and was promoted two ranks. He had turned his life around.

In 2013, I met Tom right before he and his hiking partner, veteran Adam Bautz, began their first thru-hike on the Appalachian Trail. At the time, Tom worked retail at an outdoor outfitting store in his hometown of Lewisburg, Pennsylvania. After six months spent hiking the AT, Tom had returned to a job at Appalachian Outdoors, a store in State College, surrounded by backpacking and camping gear. He went from living outside and using all that gear to working inside eight hours a day, selling it to others who were going to get out and use it themselves, which he found frustrating. Tom enjoyed his job and coworkers, but "being indoors needed to end, and end fast."

After another month of work, he gave his two weeks' notice. He got rid of most of his possessions, put the rest in storage, moved out of his home, ditched his vehicle—all in an effort to downsize and live simply. He wanted to continue hiking long distance. "I am not the kind of person who has the patience to wait years and years for the things I desire," he said. "I knew that if I wanted to make a life of this, I needed to find a way to make a name for myself so that I could, hopefully, one day make a living by backpacking."

OVER THE NEXT FEW YEARS, TOM ACCOMPLISHED A LOT. HE COMPLETED the 3,100-mile Continental Divide Trail (CDT), 600 miles of the Florida

Trail, half of the 2,600-mile Pacific Crest Trail (PCT), the 500-mile Colorado Trail, and the 800-mile Arizona Trail. In 2016 he set out for another thru-hike on the Appalachian Trail, this time in the dead of winter. As we had in 2013, Todd and I rendered some trail magic to him, for ten nights straight when Tom came through Pennsylvania. Every morning, we dropped him off at a trailhead and every evening we picked him up, fifteen to twenty-five miles farther along the trail. He enjoyed the warmth of our living room woodstove, delicious organic dinners, and fresh-baked pie and ice cream for dessert. Lounging on our sofa in the evenings, he made himself comfortable. During this time we really got to know Tom, and he became family.

Tom had chosen a winter trek on the AT for multiple reasons. "This hike was about conquering a fear I had of backpacking in the winter alone in harsh conditions." He had only hiked in the summer and wondered, "Can I succeed and not die out there?" Tom didn't see a single footprint in all 280-plus miles of Maine. Although the AT is the most traveled, highly populated trail in the United States, he didn't encounter another long-distance backpacker until he reached Pennsylvania. "I'm hiking in the winter because I need risk in my life," he explained. "I get the adrenaline rush I grew used to feeling in the military which seems normal." He realized that hiking in the winter made him happy. "It makes me feel alive. The risk is worth the reward if I can overcome it. It is better than living a dull life."

With every step, Tom learned to make peace with pain. He hiked more than three hundred miles on stress fractures, and dozens of miles on torn cartilage in his knee after a hundred-foot fall on an icy trail. "I'm also hiking through the winter to be alone with myself," he said. "Every single day it is just me. There is nothing to distract me from myself. In the Marine Corps, we are taught to internalize many things. Walking helps me process things. I miss my Marine buddies. I lost forty guys. I don't have any regrets about what I did over there. I had suicidal thoughts *before* the Marines. The Marines gave me the opportunity to change my course: one hundred percent I would be dead or in jail without them."

For Tom, the winter journey along the AT was the culmination of a long-distance-hiking lifestyle that had evolved from his passion into an occupation and a new identity. Back in 2013, the farther along the trail he progressed, the more he fell in love with the hiking life. The simplicity and freedom are what he loves most. "Hiking really appeals to me because there is something very special about experiencing a new place on foot at a speed of two to three miles per hour," he said. "When you walk through land for months, you absorb so much more of it. It becomes part of you. You have a connection to it. You get rooted, so to speak." The winter hike made him learn to appreciate everything. He saw beauty everywhere and learned to feel gratitude. He embraced all that the winter wilderness threw at him—darkness, pain, and loneliness. He was experiencing the gifts of peacetime living—beauty, gratitude, new things. "My worst day on the trail," Tom said, "is still better than my best back in normal society."

TOM GOT HIS START ON THE APPALACHIAN TRAIL IN 2013, BUT IT WASN'T until he hiked the Continental Divide Trail the following year that he realized he had fallen in love with wilderness. "All the pieces started to fit, and I felt truly at peace. It was a magical experience that I will always cherish as being a coming-of-age moment for myself. Lewisburg will always be home to me, but the trails now feel like my new home." His love of movement pushes him to constantly crave different scenes, which the trail provides:

> On the trail I experience an overwhelming feeling of fullness—the fullness of life, the feeling that I am where I am supposed to be, doing exactly what I am supposed to be doing, like looking at a view that only God could have made just for me in that specific moment in time. I experience so many good things and so many bad things all at once and yet stretched out over hundreds of miles and countless hours, I always seem to land on my own two feet with a smile on my face at a perfect sunset-facing vista. All the rainy, cold, exhausting, crappy twenty-mile days are worth those moments. And they are fortified by the strangers that become your lifelong friends that you are experiencing all this with.

THERE IS SCIENCE BEHIND THIS MIND-SET OF "FULLNESS" THAT TOM EXPEriences while on the trail. In addition to exercising his body, his brain is also getting a workout, according to Dr. Michael Merzenich, professor at the University of California, San Francisco, and a leading researcher in brain plasticity. In *Soft-Wired: How the New Science of Brain Plasticity Can Change Your Life*, Merzenich explains that contrary to walking on flat, even ground, navigating a hiking trail forces the mind to assess and reassess the environment. Hikers have to watch the ground to determine where to place their feet, evaluate weather, and regulate their body heat and nutrition. A hiker needs to be aware of the surrounding landscape, scan for novelty, unpredictability, surprises such as wild animal encounters, approaching storms, and so much more. To navigate a trail, a hiker must function in a super-charged state. This hyper-engagement with the environment is actually exercising the brain—the complete opposite of a life spent indoors focused on screens and electronic devices. The latter seems to breed disorders like depression and anxiety, whereas hiking in wild areas feeds both the body and the brain like vitamins.

Another ingredient that feeds the soul, of course, is strong family support. Tom's mother adores him, and Tom adores his mother. She laughed as she told stories about what a challenge he was to raise, her only hope was that he would reach his eighteenth year alive. Tom's parents and family showered him with unconditional love. Because of their active presence in his life, he was able to forgive himself when he returned home from Iraq, silence the voices that murmured in his ear, dismiss any nightmares, love himself, and move on. "I could go through hell and back, experience all kinds of horror," Tom said, "but since I have been blessed with a loving support system waiting for me back home, and have a positive outlook, I can continue to go into nature, walk and heal, and find great joy."

On Tom's winter hike along the Appalachian Trail in 2016, his probation officer jumped into his mind out of the blue. He thought about how far he had come, how good his life was now, and decided it might be fun to reach out to the officer when he returned home. When he was in jail, Tom was a clean-cut eighteen-year-old. Today, he has a long beard and even longer hair, but he has his act together. More than staying out of trouble, he has succeeded professionally as a long-distance hiker and created a brand for himself as "the Real Hiking Viking." He has served as a Trail Ambassador and a gear tester. To his surprise, when Tom finally reached the probation officer on the phone, the officer asked, "Is this the *Real* Hiking Viking?" He had been following Tom's adventures and success on Facebook and Instagram for years!

Not long ago, Tom serendipitously ran into the judge who sentenced him. Everyone in the system supposedly disliked the short, elderly woman for doling out tough-love sentences. Tom told the judge all the good things that he had accomplished since jail. "I believe that jail was the best thing that ever happened to me," he said. "It moved me in the right direction. I knew I could do more with my life. You gave me that chance and I want to thank you from the bottom of my heart." The judge appeared shocked that Tom approached her and shared his message, but she was equally shocked, in a pleasant way, that he had benefitted so positively from her sentence.

From jail to life in the Marines to finding peace on the trail, it hasn't always been easy, but Tom has some advice for other veterans: "No matter what you are struggling with in life, you can find peace in the outdoors. You may not ever fully heal from whatever issues you are having, whether it is post-traumatic stress, moral injury, or just the anxiety of everyday life. You can find a healthy break from all of this by getting outside and unplugging from the craziness that is our modern society. This life of the trail is what I need. It works for me and it could work for you. I could be happy anywhere as long as I've got my pack with me."

CHAPTER 5

ILENE HENDERSON

US ARMY, 1994–2015

AT TWENTY YEARS OLD, ILENE Henderson enlisted in the US Army as a counterintelligence agent, completed the US Army Airborne School, and qualified as "expert" on several weapons. In her late twenties, she attended a motorcycle racing school, got licensed, and raced motorcycles with the Western Eastern Roadracing Association (WERA), one of a few women in the organization at the time. She can drink Jack Daniel's with the best of them. She is beautiful with a killer smile and a bright light in her eyes.

During her twenty-one years of service in the Army, she deployed three times—to Haiti in 1996, to combat in Afghanistan in 2003–2004, and again to Iraq in 2006–2007. As a counterintelligence agent, she served as a member of a four-person tactical human-intelligence team. She recruited and ran local sources, collecting intelligence and developing target packets. She was at the top of her game in Iraq in 2007 when the bottom of her world fell out. Her appendix ruptured, releasing toxins into her abdominal cavity. She was medevaced out and almost died as a result of an infection and ensuing complications. After four surgeries in four months, Ilene's illness left residual trauma in her stomach. She did not know it at the time, but she had contracted a harmful *Escherichia coli (E. coli)* infection while in Afghanistan in 2003, which had lain dormant until her appendix ruptured. She recalled:

I had never been in the hospital before, never been that close to death, even in a war zone. I was never faced with that kind of physiological challenge.

The military judges you objectively. There are established standards, and your worth as a soldier is determined by whether you meet the standards. I was used to being judged and validated by my level of physical fitness and weapons qualifications. I had always been a successful soldier, easily passing my physical fitness tests and qualifying expert on my assigned weapons. After my appendix ruptured, I struggled to meet the physical fitness standards. I felt like a failure as a soldier.

In contrast, the civilian world is subjective. As a woman you are judged by the size of your boobs, how pretty you are, how nice of a home you own, whether you have a boyfriend or husband, and how many kids you have. I am not arm candy or a trophy wife. At forty years old, I had no boyfriend or husband, owned no home, had no kids. I felt like a failure as a woman.

LIFE AFTER WAR WAS NOT EASY FOR ILENE. LIKE MANY COMBAT VETERANS, she returned from her deployments a different person and had a hard time acclimating back into society. She was used to the chaos of a war zone, not automobile traffic and the seemingly petty behavior of civilians. "I left part of my soul in Afghanistan and Iraq," she said. "On some level, I felt more at home over there. In this civilian world, in this society, I did not fit in at all." Ilene returned to college to finish her degree but found she had little in common with the students. She felt angry and was extremely short-tempered. She gained more weight. She felt understood only by her own tribe, her fellow military comrades who had the same mindset.

As women veterans transition to civilian life, they face unique challenges compounded by a lack of female-veteran community. According to the data from the Department of Veterans Affairs, more than thirty thousand women leave the military every year. There are about two million women veterans in America and Puerto Rico. Their trauma is often further compounded by the sexual abuse that they experience while in the military. In *Struggle Well: Thriving in the Aftermath of Trauma*, authors Ken Falke and Josh Goldberg say that "[veterans'] problems have a lot more to do with what they are coming home to, rather than what they are coming back from. The military teaches men and women how to be Soldiers, but no one teaches them how to live a meaningful and productive life out of uniform." Ilene's experience back home was full of struggle. When she was involved in a car crash, hit from behind, she felt like she had been hit by an IED. Then she lost two comrades to post-deployment suicides. As she struggled to physically, mentally, and emotionally recover from her combat experiences, she knew she needed to get far away from civilian life.

Ilene recalled a conversation she had with another soldier who had successfully hiked the entire Appalachian Trail. His experiences of long-distance hiking planted a seed, and the possibility of hiking 2,180 miles thrilled her. Ilene's mother, Inga, had introduced her daughter to the natural world at a young age. The family often traveled to their cabin on seventy-five acres in the hills and hollers of southeast Missouri. Ilene spent vacations hiking, paddling, and camping. She already knew how much peace the natural world can provide a soul. "I longed to get away and clear my head," she said. "I wanted to reset after all the craziness of war and combat. I was also trying to reconnect with humanity. Hiking the Appalachian Trail seemed like a great way to relax, unwind, catch my breath, and heal, so I asked Mom, 'Do you want to do this?'"

At the time, Inga was still trying to find her place after her husband had passed. Ilene, being the oldest child, felt a responsibility to care for her. The mother and daughter team were roommates and best of friends. Inga is a schoolteacher and often takes substitute-teaching jobs so she has the freedom to travel with her daughter. Ever the adventurer (like mother, like daughter), Inga did not allow her age at the time, sixty-five, to deter her. She was game. Ilene received a fat check from the military for back pay, and both women cashed in their IRAs to fund what is typically a five- to six-month trek. They set out to thru-hike the trail together in March 2014, heading north from Georgia, taking the trail names "Hendo" and "Hendo's Mom." (Most thru-hikers assume a trail name, a new personality that often is given to a hiker, not chosen. It often describes them or something they have done and is used throughout their hike, all in fun.)

In addition to seeking her own sense of peace, Ilene wanted to help her fellow veterans. To spread the word about the crisis of veteran suicide, the pair hiked in the name of Stop Soldier Suicide, the first national civilian not-for-profit organization dedicated to preventing soldier and veteran suicide. Before Ilene even set foot on the trail, just labeling herself a thru-hiker gave her a renewed sense of purpose—she was committed to a huge goal, no matter how challenging it would be or how long it would take. Over the course of eighteen months, Ilene and her mother walked, crawled, trudged, and snowshoed 2,190 miles. They were only able to hike three and a half miles the first day and averaged six miles per day for the first two months.

Soon after beginning the hike, Ilene noticed an attitude change. "I came to grips with retiring from the military. Before that, I saw it as quitting. After hiking a while, I didn't see it as quitting but that I had completed my mission. Hiking the entire AT was my next new mission." When it came to the military, Ilene felt self-conscious and insecure, but she felt worthy on the trail, where "no one cares if you are male or female. You are not negatively judged or considered less-than. It is about how far you have hiked. This is something that I can do (thru-hike). Out here, I am a success."

Because they went so slowly, winter arrived. The pair had to get a little creative to continue the hike over the year and a half that it took them to complete it. In New England they were up to their waists in snow, on snowshoes, wearing microspikes to navigate ice. In some places, the trail blazes were few and difficult to follow. They had to sleep in minus-zero temps. "I'm not going to quit just because it's fuckin' winter," Ilene said. "With snowshoes, it is do-able. You *can* take more than six months to hike the AT. I'm going to see it through to the end." Hiking with her mom made it much more fun "to share the suck with someone." They had the same mentality on the trail: get up and put in your miles every day. Both women gave it their all. "We never *both* had a bad day on the trail on the same day," she remembered. "We took turns being down and also being the cheerleader."

There were a few times when they sat down and had a serious conversation about how they could possibly continue. There were multiple reasons to quit: they were running out of money, Ilene had Army Reserve training to complete, and they needed to drive to North Carolina and move their belongings out of their rental house because they were being evicted. These setbacks made quitting seem easier and staying on the trail more challenging. In the face of each challenge, they reviewed all options, strategized, and ultimately decided to keep going. They thought creatively about how to avoid the worst of winter in the high northern mountains. They took Inge's car out of storage, and she slack-packed Ilene through some of the challenging mountain miles. Inge would drop her daughter at a trailhead, and Ilene would snowshoe alone. Then her mother would park the car at the next road crossing and snowshoe in from the opposite end to meet Ilene. They enlisted the help of many "trail angels" who gave them a warm place to stay in their home, a hearty meal, and assisted with shuttles. As it has for many other hiking veterans, the Appalachian Trail helped Ilene find a new tribe. Meeting all the great people—other hikers and trail angels—was very reassuring. "I never thought I'd find a group of people who were not military, who could be my friends, where I would fit in."

ILENE FINISHED THE AT ON NOVEMBER 23, 2015, TWENTY MONTHS AFTER she began and with eighteen months of hiking. This date was close to the anniversary of when she had been medevaced out of Iraq in 2007. The mother-daughter pair returned the next spring so Inga could fill in the stretches she missed while shuttling her daughter. She too would achieve "2,000-Miler" status. "We should get the award for the slowest thru-hikers and the ones who were at it the longest!" Ilene said. "I realized, *anyone* can hike the whole AT if you just refuse to quit. I also didn't feel like I was finishing the AT. I felt like I was starting the rest of my life."

Ilene saw definite changes in herself after her 2,180-mile trek. "On the trail, I had time to think and understand. It was a slow evolution. The miles and the hiking helped to strip away my ego. Aggression gets instilled in you in the military, but on the trail, I could focus on something peaceful and gentle like looking for wildflowers. I definitely think my mental health is better now. I am not nearly as angry or bitter. I have learned that anger is a waste of time and your life." Ilene's mother agreed and said she has seen a big positive change in her daughter. "She doesn't blow up nearly as much," Inga said, "and has more tolerance and patience, as well as visible inner peace."

The natural environment promotes a "love of life" attitude called biophilia. A growing body of scientific research suggests that the human brain craves green environments and wild places. Peter Kahn, a professor of psychology in the School of Environmental and Forest Sciences at the University of Washington, and the late Stephen Kellert, a professor at Yale University's School of the Environment, studied this affinity. The human brain actually prefers natural scenery to artificial structures and surroundings. "I feel better, too," Ilene goes on. "I lost a lot of weight and even though I'm not the physical badass I once was, I'm still a badass in other ways." When Ilene was deployed, she was in the best shape of her life and at her most confident. Ever since, she has been trying to get back that feeling of high self-confidence, superb fitness, a deep connection to the people around her, to the world, and to herself. Hiking the AT was the first time she got close to those feelings, and after completing the long trek she again had that sense of accomplishment, purpose, and fulfillment:

> When you are in a war zone, you are aware of how quickly you can die or be killed. There is a rawness; you have a clear purpose and sense of fulfillment. The only other place I feel this way is in nature, in the outdoors, in the wilds.
>
> On the trail, I woke up every day with a purpose, a mission, to walk north. Although it was a struggle, I saw tangible progress as we covered the miles. In the military, I learned to take a big problem and break it down into small increments, piece by piece. That is how I approached the whole AT, day by day, mile by mile, not concentrating on the end goal of completion. The trail taught me that. I was able to translate what I learned in the military to the trail of life. I only wish life had blazes to help direct you.

ILENE'S REENTRY INTO SOCIETY AFTER THE HIKE INCLUDED SOME challenges. Coming back home felt like returning after her combat deployments. She felt like an alien again. She missed her trail friends like she missed her Army buddies. "In this society, I have to mentally try to stay positive and focused," she said. "It is easy when I hike. The trail placed me in the present. When I am not hiking it is easy to become full of doubt and question myself and my path through life. 'What if this doesn't work? What is the next right thing?'"

As much as the trail healed and validated Ilene, she needed a new sense of purpose, as do most returning veterans. "No matter how much time goes by and how many different experiences we have in the civilian world," she said, "we will spend the rest of our lives searching for and trying to achieve that same sense of fulfillment and purpose we had while deployed in combat. There is no greater sense of fulfillment than serving in combat. You can come close but it will never be the same."

With Ilene's vast array of construction, mechanical, electrical, and automotive skills, she purchased a vintage 1950s travel trailer and rebuilt it to be a beautiful new home for her mother and her. She continued to work to better herself, graduating from Methodist University with a bachelor's degree in history, and began applying for seasonal national park ranger jobs. Since completing the Appalachian Trail, Ilene realized how much she loved the trails and mountains, and so she sought an outdoor occupation.

Being a seasonal national park ranger held a lot of appeal for Ilene because the job shares many parallels with the military. In the military, things are always changing. People are always rotating; you have a new commander and first sergeant every twelve months. As a seasonal park ranger, she could change her place of assignment every six months. The advantages to this lifestyle are you get to live in a new location, get to know a new part of the country, learn a whole new set of skills, and have new adventures. You get to truly experience a place when you live there for six months instead of just passing through. As a staff sergeant, Ilene's job was to train soldiers. As a park ranger, she would interact with visitors, meet people from all over the world, educate and teach them how to be responsible in the natural world, care for special places that are national parks and monuments, and help visitors to understand why designated parklands should be protected. She felt that working as a park ranger could give her a renewed sense of purpose and fulfillment.

When Ilene was interviewing for a park ranger job for the upcoming summer season, a ranger at one of the positions she applied for called to discuss the details of the position and make sure she understood the responsibilities to see if she was still interested. "I explained that I felt qualified and confident in my abilities," she said. "I mentioned that during my time in the Army I had successfully completed two combat deployments, one to Afghanistan with Special Forces and one to Iraq with an Infantry company. Therefore, I was comfortable interacting with aggressive, strong-willed, and sometimes intoxicated individuals." In 2018, Ilene scored her first ranger job with the National Park Service in Jewel Cave National Monument, South Dakota.

> I have new challenges in my life now, new things happening. My hike through life continues, and when I reach a double blaze in the trail, I take the turn and head in a new direction. I am very excited. I will admit I am a lot of things and have a lot of faults. . . . I am loud, hard of hearing, a white badass woman, stubborn, passionate, biker chick, and I am attentive to detail, a good shot, I drink a lot of Jack, enjoy cigars, and many other qualities I can't think of. Take note, though, one thing I know for damn sure is that I am not in any way, shape, or form a quitter!

PART TWO

THE TRAIL
REVEALS

CHAPTER 6

TOMMY BUCCI

US ARMY, 1995–2015

WHEN TOMMY BUCCI SPEAKS, HIS rough-sounding, raspy voice is straight out of *The Godfather*. You might think he injured his larynx during one of his many deployments over his thirty-year military career. Not so. The Italian part is accurate, but his unique voice is the result of a barroom brawl when he was a young man, fresh in the Army. His chin was not tucked and a punch delivered to his throat created scar tissue on his larynx. He also did a lot of screaming throughout his military career (finished at the rank of command sergeant major), which did not help matters.

Tommy doesn't swing his fists anymore, but he still doesn't take any shit. He hails from the blue-collar town of Norristown, along Pennsylvania's Schuylkill River. As a boy, he loved to play in the woods, shoot guns, and blow up stuff. Many of his relatives were in the construction business. At a young age, Tommy learned how to build things and how to fix the things he and others built. He labored for a masonry construction company during his summers while in high school. When he joined the Army, it was a natural assumption that he would excel at construction, but he also branched out into infantry, mortars, land navigation, mechanics, first aid, civil affairs, paratrooping—whatever there was a need for. In the military he took classes and went back to school to learn these skills and more.

In Iraq and Afghanistan, among other countries, he was in charge of building and engineering much of the infrastructure our military used to operate. Tommy also helped the locals with their own construction projects, such as roads, sanitation, and plumbing. He accomplished all his jobs while the war went on around him with small-arms exchanges, shells flying by, and mortars exploding. Because of his extensive training in Infantry, Army units would send Tommy out to build things without fear of him being a defenseless liability; he was able to function in combat. This brought Tommy into many hostile scenarios. These types of physical jobs and functioning in a high-stress environment came easy to him, and in fact Tommy thrived. He ran on adrenaline—"ate it every day like vitamins," he said. Today, at fifty-six, Tommy moves around quickly, like a lad in his twenties. Indeed, he says he has two speeds, "Fast and stop." He claims the constant movement helps lubricate his pinched nerves and compressed disks.

Tommy has many residual aches and pains resulting from beating up his body during a lifetime of active service, but you'd be hard-pressed to hear about them. Tommy explains, "I always led from the front and believed I had to be meaner, faster, stronger than all of them. Ibuprofen takes care of the aches and pains!"

IN ADDITION TO THE PHYSICAL PAIN, TOMMY HAS SOME RESIDUAL ANGER issues left over from his wartime experience. The anger, he said, was necessary to perform as a successful soldier. Anger and aggression are the stuff that keep combat soldiers alive as well as giving them the ability to kill first. But for a lot of soldiers, that anger continues to rear its ugly head after they return home from deployment—in their marriages, relationships, job situations, and other realms. It runs deep and becomes one's personality over time. "Anger is also the only 'manly' emotion," psychologist Lynne Williams explained. "It can also cover up and 'stand in' for other emotions, like fear, doubt, guilt, because it is energizing."

In his younger days, Tommy was quick to be aggressive, not mean but certainly ready to brawl, and this behavior continued throughout his many years as an infantry fighter. During his thirty-four years in the Army, he served in over twenty countries and collected countless medals. Lifestyle impacts personality and vice versa. Tommy admits to still being a bit aggressive underneath. As time passed and he grew older, Tommy mellowed and eventually gravitated to the big outdoors. His love of nature goes back to his childhood. As a young boy he was a scout, and he often went hiking in the woods and paddling in the nearby lakes and rivers. But in the service, like most members, he limited his activities to running on base and lifting weights; time in nature receded into his past. In recent years, however, Tommy acquired two dogs, one a therapy dog, and one a rescue. The dogs need daily exercise, which compelled Tommy to get out with them. His dogs keep him young and fit, so everyone benefits.

Tommy first acquired Max while he was still on active duty. Max is a labradoodle, a curly-haired dog specifically bred for a hypoallergenic coat that does not shed. Max, however, does shed and is scraggly coated, so the breeder relinquished him to Tommy. The pair attended classes so Max could become Tommy's service dog. Max can sense when Tommy is starting to act "fucked up"—yelling and arguing and getting agitated. Max will alert Tommy that he is behaving in an unhealthy manner. He and Max go everywhere together, even to work before Tommy retired from the Army. "Service dogs," according to Kevin Ferris and Dava Guerin, authors of *Vets and Pets, Wounded Warriors and the Animals That Help Them Heal,* "must be specifically trained to mitigate the veterans' disabilities, essentially performing tasks the veterans cannot do," including alerting and then calming them down when their behavior is becoming unruly. "Companion animals . . . though not trained to perform specific tasks . . . come in all shapes and sizes and give veterans unconditional support and love. They also help relieve anxiety, as well as mitigate panic attacks, the symptoms of PTSD, and more."

Emotional support animals—often dogs or cats—aren't trained in any specific skills; people draw support simply from their presence. Service and therapy dogs are different, as Tommy explains: "Service dogs are trained to perform specific tasks for a specific disability, like turning on lights, picking things up. Therapy dogs soothe the patient with specific behaviors that help psychologically, like leaning or lying on the owner in a panic attack, alerting behavior, and staying close." "All dogs are therapy for their owners," Tommy clarifies, "but not all dogs are therapy dogs. Dogs also retire from service since their working skills dwindle as the dog gets older. Many dogs can be service dogs; a professional trainer tests the animal for behavioral traits. For example, not every Labrador retriever can be a service dog, but when bred for service, they excel."

Tommy began his own personal journey of healing once he retired from the military. He went to his local VA hospital and said, "This, this, and this hurts. This is what is wrong with me and I need you to fix me." While visiting the VA hospital grounds, everywhere he looked the buildings were in disrepair. Tommy thought he could share his construction expertise, and so he convinced the administration to hire him. He started as a temporary electrician and worked his way up to supervisor within a year, then on to a project manager for large projects within the next year.

While on the VA campus, he witnessed all the broken veterans who were enrolled in the PTSD and drug- and alcohol-rehab programs. He noticed that their sedentary lifestyle bred more inactivity, which could make them unhealthy, overweight, and depressed. Tommy also knew that their many meds did not necessarily clean up their emotional mess and sometimes contributed to it. Recreating outdoors with a dog, however, was Tommy's new miracle pill for healing, and he wanted to share it with the veterans in the rehab programs.

Tommy enrolled the two of them in a training program so Max could become a certified pet therapy dog. Tommy began bringing Max into the PTSD ward on a weekly basis to let the vets interact with him. He noticed that his dog visits brought out more joy in the vets' lives than anything else. "Speaking from experience, I know what works for me—moving in nature and being with my dog. This dog is my therapy, my serotonin, my oxytocin, my reason for doing things outdoors in nature. It keeps him happy and it keeps me happy. Max is the reason I am *not* in the rehab program at the veterans' hospital. Dogs can heal veterans in areas where the VA can't."

AFTER TOMMY RETIRED FROM THE MILITARY, HE SHIFTED HIS FOCUS TO helping his men get better. In 2016, Tommy began his nonprofit, Soldier Sanctuary: Healing Through Outdoor Therapy. He is paying it forward. Soldier Sanctuary is specialized: Tommy, a combat vet, is helping other combat vets. He sticks to small groups of four to five men, a "fire team," no matter the branch. He attempts to re-create the same spirit of how such a small team sticks together through the best and worst of times, with no judgment, political correctness, or inhibitions. The nonprofit operates right out of Tommy's pickup because it can fit five people, five bikes, five boats, and five sets of camping gear all at once, as he leads his veterans into healing nature. His organization's motto carries the acronym GTFO (Get the Fuck Outside). He just wants the men to move, to come outside and away from their video games, and fight the depression and post-traumatic stress, which so many struggle with. Depression can lead to no motivation and no desire for formerly pleasurable things.

If anyone can move and shake these men, it is Tommy Bucci. He takes vets and his dogs out canoeing and hiking on a very impressive schedule. In 2017, Soldier Sanctuary put on 123 events, and the following year, 141. They paddle the Schuylkill River, hike the trails in the county's surrounding parks, and ride bikes among the military monuments in Washington, DC. The healing improves and deepens exponentially with the help of Max and Tommy's second dog, a Dutch shepherd named Gino, who was bred to be a working dog by American K9. This organization trains dogs to work in drug detection, law enforcement, customs and border patrol, and wars. Gino's training was for patrol and explosive detection, not as a pet. His two-year program began when he was very young. He learned to identify the odors in explosives—propellants, igniters, ammonia, and so on. Upon detection, Gino would lie down near the explosive.

The shepherd spent five years working in Afghanistan and was retired at age seven, when many military dogs typically lose interest and might instead get aggressive. Gino was acquired by K9 Hero Haven in Herndon, Pennsylvania. This nonprofit began in 2015 to serve the military, veterans, and first responders by adopting out retired working dogs after interviewing and matching the prospective owner with the dogs' personalities. The nonprofit is operated by husband-and-wife team Anne and Mike Gibbs, both Iraq war veterans. "They are one of the best in the country," Tommy says. "Their dogs were rescued from the war where they served as military service dogs, and now they rescue wounded warriors as pet therapists." Today, Gino is twelve years old, and Tommy has had him for four years.

In *Vets and Pets*, the authors explain that "since some companions come from the many animal shelters that pair vets and pets, the newly formed teams share one thing in common—a new lease on life. The veteran now has help overcoming emotional obstacles, and the animal is saved from loneliness or worse." When the Gibbs received Gino, he was deemed "dangerous" and had a history of attacking his handlers. "He just needed love and positive reinforcement," Tommy assured, "And he needs to run." Tommy takes Gino and Max on daily runs, and they enter races where they run right by their master's side. And, of course, the dogs go with Tommy and the vets on every canoe ride and hike.

In the VA's PTSD unit, Tommy's dogs take over like they own the ward, running up and down the hallway, thrilled to see the men and have them pet them and play with them. "It's not the way a service dog is supposed to behave—overly friendly," Tommy explained. "But their behavior is perfect for healing these guys. If someone comes up to pet them, their bodies wiggle in anticipation." Therapy dogs are expected to behave a certain way, and they are exponentially better when they are wearing their working vests, but Tommy's dogs definitely march to their own drummer. The veterans love his dogs, and Tommy speaks the language of the vets. "I tell the vets, 'I am going to go play outside with these dogs, with or without you, so you may as well take the opportunity and come along.'" He knows firsthand what published studies in *Scientific American* have concluded: "Like chatting with a good friend, interacting with dogs increases levels of neurotransmitters such as oxytocin and dopamine that promote positive emotions and bonding."

I HAD THE OPPORTUNITY TO GO FOR A PADDLE WITH TOMMY AND HIS DOGS on nearby Chambers Lake, in Chester County, Pennsylvania—a favorite destination of the veterans enrolled in VA programs where Tommy works. Tommy held the boat stable and helped Gino and Max climb onboard. The dogs were very curious, lapping water off the side of the boat, sniffing the air and the nearby bank, and basically waiting to get where they could run and play. Tommy's usual procedure is to load the vets into his boats and lead them across the lake to narrow Birch Run, which feeds the lake. The channel narrows to an intimate passage that encourages a wilderness exploration. We pulled over at the creek's mouth and unloaded onto a large flat rock for a break. Tommy told me more about his life as a soldier and what caused him the most angst after his long career in the military.

In the Middle East wars, Tommy's main job was construction engineer while "winning the hearts and minds of the Iraqi and Afghan people," he said. Tom would meet with the local officials, the sheikhs, and the chiefs, and with a massive budget doled out by the US military, was able to ask, "What do you need to improve your life? A road? A well?" He couldn't spend the money fast enough. Tommy handed out candy and stuffed animals to their children, and everywhere he went he was cheered, greeted warmly, and invited into homes for meals.

Tommy was proactive about learning the language, taking classes and buying books, but he always had an interpreter along who knew the local dialect. While doing his work, he got to know the locals, and was able to distinguish between the good guys and bad guys.

The message he delivered, Tom told me, was that America wants to make you independent and strong. The interpreters were happy to help as they too wanted their country stable and safe for their families, and Tommy grew close to them all. Doing this important work, however, Tommy was always a target. He had a price on his head. "I knew I was buying their love." But the interpreters, Tommy later found out, had to pay an even higher price for their involvement. Five times during one deployment, Tommy's superiors extracted him from one village and sent him on to another mission or project. "We were doing such great things but then I'd get moved. The families of the interpreters were threatened, kidnapped, held hostage, or murdered. This happened over and over again—wiping out the families of those who trusted us. We created this monster," Tommy admitted.

People in their villages were supposed to follow up and continue doing the good work the American soldiers had begun, but the bad guys would move in after Tom and his men left. "These were good people. They did not want power or money. These guys were PhDs—doctors and educators. They expected the US military to provide safety and security for them and their families like we promised, but the bad element was stronger than anyone had anticipated." Tom has survivor's guilt and sadness about what happened to these people. "I know what all these guys are doing in the PTSD ward. I know how they feel and what they are dealing with since they have returned, and I want to share the healing that the outdoors and my dogs can bring."

ALTHOUGH HE HAS A FABULOUS PROGRAM, TOMMY DID NOT EXPECT TO find the challenges he faces in Soldier Sanctuary. He didn't think motivation would be that difficult for so many of the guys he tries to help who are young and in good shape. Tom thought that when they were back with "the boys" again in his organization's tight-knit, small "fire teams," the camaraderie would return to their lives. He believed they would find strength in the natural world as they sobered up in the VA program and got pumped up to begin anew. Tommy spent a lot of money on canoes and kayaks for his non-profit, purchased backpacking gear, raised money, and acquired sponsors. He hoped to mentor a few vets on a long-distance hike on the Appalachian Trail for maximum healing, but "it's feast or famine," he said. "Sometimes one or two show up for an outing, sometimes ten. I was completely unprepared for the laziness that exists in the ward. Depression, PTSD, lack of motivation—it's a continuous triangle of unhealthy behavior."

When he does get the vets to come out, they "may bitch and moan, but they go home afterward having had a great time." He said, "I pick them up and take them back. I pay for everything. I take them out to dinner. No drinking or drugs is allowed." He gives out participant gifts when the vets attend, like Soldier Sanctuary mugs, high-quality T-shirts, sticky notes, sometimes jackets—all veteran produced, along with copies of a little book that he considers excellent, *Anxiety and Depression for Dummies*. Tommy has found that although many of the veterans who graduate from the VA's rehab program begin to make healthy life choices, stay clean, and remain sober for a while, some relapse and slide back into the program. These are his stories:

> I get more fucked up from these guys relapsing than my own PTSD. They have my cell. They call me at all hours of the night. They relapse. They get in trouble. They get thrown into jail. It breaks my heart. I didn't save them, I didn't heal them, but I helped them. See, I get them. I am one of them. I really think that years in a lifestyle where adrenaline is kicking in all the time, changes something in your body and your brain. It fucks you up, for life. But I know this way of recreating in the outdoors helps every damn time. This stuff is as old as time. I didn't invent anything.
>
> I've been doing this rehab work for six years now and it didn't take long to pinpoint what these vets really need to heal—nature and that same tight-knit bond that they had in the military. It

worked for me and it will work for them. I say to them, "Let's do it. Let's do it together. We're all in this together." That's what the military is—camaraderie. I want to heal them all. One vet said to me, "Dude, I haven't felt this good in years. You've done more for me than any doctor. [This particular vet hadn't spoken for a week to anyone in the program until Tommy got him outside.] There is something in the outdoors that helps. Playing with the dogs in the woods makes me feel so much better. In that environment, I don't think about combat and the losses."

I was a leader in the Army. Now, I motivate and lead veterans in a different, better way. I may be the one who caused some of their emotional problems (or commanders like me). I always felt that it would be good for me to give back. Soldier Sanctuary gives me the opportunity to take care of soldiers again, and this type of care is ten times better than the military's care. I might have grown up in the city, as well as many of these veterans, but outside, in the woods, on the trails, in the water, I feel very different. I feel very good and I want these hurting vets to feel good again too.

CHAPTER 7

MARIO KOVACH

US AIR FORCE, 1998–2018

ONE OF FIRST THINGS YOU notice when you meet Mario Kovach is his forearms. Not just the impressive muscles, but more the names tattooed all over them. There is a story behind each name. Because Mario served twenty years in the military, you can assume that the stories are probably pretty sad. His arms bear the names of the twenty Air Force explosive ordnance disposal (EOD) technicians killed in combat operations in the Iraq and Afghan wars from improvised explosive devices or suicide bombers. Mario knew most of them. An EOD technician's job is to mitigate the effects of any explosives to protect both personnel and property. As a retired Air Force master sergeant, Mario spent twenty years as an EOD team member and team leader.

Mario did not thrive in college and after a couple of semesters at Penn State, he felt he needed more direction. The Air Force appealed to him as he looked for discipline and structure. He flipped to the back of the job description booklet provided by the recruiter and found the special forces information. Mario recalls that as a youth, he would blow up apples with firecrackers. He was always fascinated with explosives, but he did not dream of a career in the military. As he read the description he thought an EOD bomb technician did some pretty cool stuff, including presidential-support missions. He had an imaginative mind and enjoyed taking things apart to see how they worked. Such qualities are necessary attributes for carrying out this dangerous job, so it was a good fit. Mario signed up in 1998 when the whole world was experiencing heightened security awareness.

EOD work is the epitome of critical dynamic thinking. It all comes down to the ability to think outside the box, on your feet. You take the information you get from the situation and interpret it using all available technological data as well as your own critical thinking and evaluation skills. EOD technicians must have a clear understanding of how things work so they know what action to take. The EOD technician trains constantly in military munitions, which are any piece of military explosives or weapons. They read the intelligence reports to see what is the most common explosive used where their mission will be carried out. Then they basically build it and re-create the scenario. They recreated the Boston Marathon bomb and trained on that. Mario trained on the bombs that Ted Kaczynski made as the Unabomber—the lone American bomber who terrorized the nation for nearly twenty years, planting mail bombs that killed three Americans and injured many more.

AFTER THE POST-9/11 WARS BEGAN IN IRAQ AND AFGHANISTAN, THE IMPRO-vised explosive device became the weapon of choice in the Middle East. The EOD technicians obtained many of these captured homemade bombs so they could examine and dismantle them, and then build replicas for in-theater EOD training. Mario trained and worked in North Dakota, South Korea, Italy, Arizona, England, and finally in New Jersey. He took care of any explosive hazard on his base and often supported the Secret Service during presidential and VIP visits. Most of his work was during combat deployments supporting sister service units. Fourteen of his twenty years of active duty were during war, and it took a toll on Mario. His whole adult life had been spent with bombs.

"You get hyperfocused," he recalled about the work. "You call on your muscle memory to perform and your training automatically kicks in. There is nothing in your head but the task at hand. When you put on your gas mask or your bomb suit, it feels as if you are losing brain cells. It is a little harder to think while wearing it. The suit weighs eighty-five to ninety pounds and it is very difficult to maneuver in it. You are confined and restricted and it is hot. A fan in your helmet cools your head and tries to keep the lens from getting fogged up, but you're going to sweat anyway." Despite all this, Mario really enjoyed his work. He loved the critical thinking aspect of it. "Guys like me thrive in crisis situations. But the longer you are in combat, the more your nature begins to change. Our wires get crossed. You might be in a mall at home on leave, but hypervigilance mode is going through the roof. I feel as if I have to pay close attention to details and I can't turn it off in a normal situation. We don't have a switch. For so long and for so often, I needed to keep the team alive. Urgency becomes the norm. This lifestyle has completely eroded my nerves."

When Mario is with his family, they are his "team." He views his family like he's leading his EOD team on a mission (this is his illogical side). "In normal life, if we are getting ready to go away as a family and my wife or kids forget something and goes back inside, I completely blow the situation out of proportion. I behave as if I am throwing a temper tantrum. I have been on so many calls when things did not go according to plan. I had so much pressure to take care of the job at hand and the possible catastrophic consequences. There was only a certain amount of time to do the job."

ONE OF THE ONLY WAYS THAT MARIO CAN COME CLOSE TO RELAXING IS going out into nature. All the noise of daily life along with the responsibilities just melt away. "I was so used to war, chaos, death, destruction—basic evil shit. When I look at nature, the rolling hills of Pennsylvania, the trees, the rivers, I think to myself, 'I love this.' I would love to go out in it and just walk, for days. Nature is so pure and undisturbed. Man has not fucked it up. Being out there represents a simpler time for me. I can focus on what is happening in the natural world, right now, and not be concerned about the future."

Mario enjoyed the outdoors as a kid and young adult. He grew up enjoying the outdoors with his family, going to the local state park, hiking, mountain biking, rock climbing and repelling. While living on base in New Jersey and between deployments, he began to remember the important and beneficial connection he had with nature. The home his family rented was on five acres, and the landlord gave Mario permission to do things like build a treehouse for his boys and put up a zipline. It was a way to incorporate the outdoors with his children.

Mario liked the military lifestyle of moving frequently, but after so many years he grew tired of being away from his family. To properly lead his team, he had to be away for long stretches. His wife, Becca, like so many military wives, essentially became a single parent on the weekends. Then Mario began having to travel to DC more frequently for Secret Service support, which caused his schedule to become even more chaotic, and the family could not plan anything. Since New Jersey is centrally located between Philadelphia, Washington, DC, and New York City, Mario and his team were some of the first to be called for special support. Mario missed a lot of family time with his job, like the boys' first steps, holidays, birthdays.

During Mario's third deployment in 2008–2009, his dresser—an old explosive container—was adorned with pictures of his family. "I had this intense desire to reach through the photograph and get a hug from them. I felt a huge lack and loss in my life." It got worse after his fourth deployment in 2011 when he and his extended family were vacationing in Spain. His family began to notice changes in Mario, and they were not good ones. Mario did not pay attention to his family but was doing other things. For example, when they were having a meal at an outdoor restaurant, Mario would memorize license plate numbers of cars going by as a way of being hypervigilant in case something happened. His family became frustrated and angry with him. "I was at the end of my rope for five years," he said. "I just tied a knot on the end of it and hung on."

After Mario's fifth deployment, it was obvious to him and everyone else that he needed help. In 2012, when he returned from Afghanistan, he began to talk to health-care providers. A psychiatrist put him on medication to help with his symptoms. Mario then went to Walter Reed National Military Medical Center for special sessions, which included alternative practices like yoga, Reiki, acupuncture, and mindfulness. Mindfulness works best for Mario, a breathing technique similar to the one used in meditation. It helps with regaining focus, homing in on the task at hand, and reducing stress. According to studies published in the journal *Progress in Brain Research*, the military now teaches mindfulness to help special forces operators make command decisions in chaotic times as well as find success treating PTSD. Mario tries to assume his breathing techniques when he feels anxiety coming on.

> I can explain what happens to my sympathetic and parasympa-
> thetic nervous system when I begin to go off the rails. There are two

people in me/my car. There is a driver and a passenger. The driver is logical—the cool, collected Mario who is driving most of the time. In the passenger seat is the irrational person who is a by-product of all this combat stuff. Normally, the logical Mario is driving and is in control of the steering wheel. But when certain situations present themselves, the two characters switch seats and I start driving irrationally. My logical side can see what I am seeing, but it can't do anything about it. It depends on how fast things happen. If I can remember to breathe for a split second, I increase my chances of not having the situation spiral out of control.

After he got his service dog, a Belgian Malinois named Bunker, Mario took him on walks two to three times a day, at least one mile each time. Bunker is a high-driving, high-energy dog who needs a lot of love and exercise. The pair would hop on the nearby New Jersey Batona Trail in the Pine Barrens every chance they got. "I just like to throw on my ruck like Forrest Gump and take off down the trail. It is the best feeling in the world to not be concerned about time or distance or direction, to just wander in the forest." The Malinois breed is known to be very intelligent, with strong protective and territorial instincts. They are often employed in the military and in law enforcement. Under the Americans with Disabilities Act, certified service dogs are trained to mitigate a specific problem. In Mario's case, Bunker helps him deal with anxiety—he can interpret Mario's behavioral signals and will act accordingly. Bunker needs appropriate play and mental work, so he doesn't become bored and lose focus as a service dog.

Recently Mario and Becca bought Becca's childhood home in upstate New York as their retirement home. Mario wanted to develop a plan. He knew an EOD guy who, fifteen days after his retirement, took his life. "I am huge fan of learning from history and others' mistakes," he said. "I don't do well with idle time. That's when demons get ahold of me." Mario's long-term goal is to get off his meds.

IN JULY 2019, MARIO MADE ONE OF HIS RETIREMENT DREAMS COME TRUE by completing a long-distance backpacking trip. He hiked Pennsylvania's eighty-five-mile forested Susquehannock Trail system (STS) in the mountains, camping along the way, alone without Bunker, who was getting older. The hike was a kind of experiment. Mario wanted to put himself in a situation where he could let go of all responsibilities, worries, and stresses. "This was a completely different situation for me. I am so used to working as a team, with the EOD team and with my family. I have been constantly aware of others' welfare and health, watching everything around me at all times, looking for potential danger. I wanted to go to a place that was far away from anything man-made. It had to be remote, where I would not be camping ten feet from my family or near an airport where I'd hear planes overhead." He wanted to see if he could go back to that time before he became stressed and hypervigilant. "Not a single part of me on that hike felt as if I were on a mission. I was *not* teleported back to the mountains of Afghanistan. My old irrational passenger did say, 'Fuck that, I am not going on that hike,' but he was left behind in the car."

This was very odd for Mario. He had not been in a situation for more than twenty years where he was not worrying. He normally felt he had multiple people's lives in his hands and had to protect someone from something. "To be honest, I knew the very first night that my experiment would work." The first day, after he had hiked about six miles, in the late afternoon he found a nice campsite with a campfire ring, in some pines, with rocks leaning against each other like a field recliner. He hung up his pack, set up his hammock between two trees, made dinner, lit a cigar, and settled in for the night. He was very comfortable and tried to meditate using his mindfulness and breathing techniques, which slowed his breathing way down. He became so calm and was breathing so slowly that he put himself into an altered state. Then an interesting thing happened. "It suddenly felt as if I was in a sunrise," he recalled. "My eyes were closed but there was incredible brightness on the other side of my lids. I opened my eyes to make sure it wasn't someone's flashlight, but darkness had already fallen in the forest. I closed my eyes again and the sunrise returned. I felt pure joy. It felt like the complete opposite end of the spectrum from all the bad stuff I had felt for decades." He smiled, then actually giggled. The sun faded away and the intense feeling of joy tapered off, but he slept very well that night.

As the miles and days clicked by, Mario felt a change occurring. He became even more relaxed, he could let go and really experience being out there. In the last twenty years, he had rarely gone anywhere in his life without a plan that had him in control. Mario had to be on top of every aspect, but on the trail he was able to maintain easy, joyful elatedness. "I loved, loved, loved walking through the natural world. I listened to the creek singing, and the frogs croaking, and the wind in the trees, and I watched the trees sway overhead. It was really something to be by myself without seeing another human or an airplane. No guns went off, no explosions." Toward the end of his weeklong hike, Mario's thoughts turned to larger goals like the Appalachian Trail. He's considering hiking it when the kids are off to college.

As soon as Mario returned home, Becca saw a change in him. She said, "He argued less with the kids, and didn't shout as much. He was mellow. He was able to regain the joy and happiness he had before his twenty years of military service. Mario discovered that "he may not be as completely broken as the VA says he is."

In his retirement, Mario was "scared shitless" of going the med route as a way of getting better, because he had seen the detrimental effects medications had on so many veterans. Hiking the STS was very healing for Mario. Time spent in the natural world along with his mindfulness exercises, his loving wife, his boys, and Bunker are his pathways to healing. Mario's hike proved that people can heal substantially in a short time if they are open to the lesson. "My wife and my kids mean the world to me," Mario said. "They are my reason for getting up every day." Add to that list, walking in the forest and mindfulness and you have Mario's complete list of proven ways to heal. For a twenty-year veteran whose specialty was bombs, that is saying a lot.

CHAPTER 8

SHAWN MURPHY

US ARMY, 1984–1990

TEN MILES WEST OF PAYSON, Arizona, between Flagstaff and Phoenix, lies the Mazatzal Wilderness. The Verde River flows through this land of red sandstone mesas, high peaks, and ancient Indian ruins. In the middle of this nearly four hundred square miles of wilderness, sits the LF Ranch (named for Leonard Fuller, the first homesteader on the property). When the wilderness was designated, this 1909 homestead was grandfathered in, so it is completely surrounded by wild land. After a ten-mile dirt-road drive from the sleepy town of Payson, the Doll Baby Trail begins. It's a four-mile walk across rough, steep terrain in the Sonoran Desert to reach the ranch. Veteran, long-distance hiker, and paddler Shawn Murphy lived there in 2018, working as a ranch hand. There was no cell service, no power lines connecting it to the outside world; it was completely off-grid. Meetings had to be prearranged, although things could change in the meantime. You left it up to trust and good luck.

Shawn sat in the shade of a huge cottonwood with his dog, Zelda. He didn't get off the ranch much because he had no vehicle and spent most of his time mending fences with his horse, Buck. He liked it that way. The eight-hundred-mile Arizona National Scenic Trail runs through the heart of this land, and the ranch offers a stop on the trail for weary thru-hikers. Shawn first learned of the ranch as a thru-hiker when he was on the Arizona Trail. The LF Ranch is run by matriarch Maryann Pratt, a descendant of the original owners. The forty-acre ranch leases thirty-seven thousand acres of public land to run their 160-head of free-range cattle. "Maryann is an ultra-tough woman," Shawn said. "She once got attacked by a mountain lion in her yard and fought it, killing it finally with a crowbar."

At the top of a rise, Shawn described the lay of the land: "Everything you see west, from the top of the wall of mountains, is ranchland." Maryann's "office" consists of a desk on the hill halfway up the mountain. The desk sits by the jeep track, hooked up to a solar collector that delivers a cell signal. She has her paper work set up there and runs her ranch from this remote spot.

Shawn summarized his trail experience. "I've hiked a lot—12,000 miles. The Pacific Crest Trail in 2012, the Continental Divide Trail in 2014, and the Arizona Trail in 2015 [all National Scenic Trails]. Also thrown into this mix of miles was a nonstop, forty-five-day paddle down the 2,320-mile Mississippi River." Shawn hiked in the summers and worked in the winters so he could hit the trail again come spring. All this traveling took place within a five-year window. Then from 2017 to 2018, he was Maryann's sole ranch hand.

SHAWN COMES FROM A MILITARY FAMILY. HIS DAD SERVED IN WORLD WAR II and Korea, and his oldest brother served in Vietnam. Shawn was eighteen when he joined the military in 1984 and served as a member of the military police for six years. He was later assigned to the Armed Forces Police Department in Fort Sam Houston and worked off-post at the San Antonio Police Station. He investigated all crimes and incidents involving military personnel off-post: homicides, suicides, accidental deaths. He worked undercover in off-limit areas, chased deserters and "AWOLs"—soldiers absent from their posts without permission but without the intention to desert. "In the city, I was called a cowboy because of my independent attitude."

Shawn drank heavily, something he learned from military culture. It was the only way he could relax, alleviate pressure, and forget. Tormented with nightmares, he felt the only way to escape them was drinking himself into oblivion. But during the day, Shawn was a very good MP. He was in the best shape of his life, was full of pride, and worked with a unit of people he respected. "But this is where it all ended," he said. "The MP motto is 'of the troops, for the troops.'" He had spent so much time training with the Army scouts that he had more friends among the grunts than in his own unit. He never had the "us vs them" mentality. "I just had an 'us' attitude," he said. "You have good cops, bad cops, asshole cops, and those that belong in jail. The MP is the same. The 'Blue Wall of Silence' is a bullshit thing."

By turning a blind eye to the criminal activity of the bad, Shawn knew, you are just as guilty of a crime as those who committed the act. But you are supposed to protect your own. "Some agents from the Criminal Investigation Department (CID) sent me 'undercover' to set up some bad MPs," he recounted. "I did my duty but committed the greatest sin a cop can do—I busted my own. The fallout was bad. I was labeled a disgrace and an embarrassment to my unit and the MP corps. I made them look bad." The consequences were struggles with broken trust and a sense of betrayal. Shawn couldn't sleep. "I was an outcast and I was pissed. I knew I would not be remaining in the military."

In 1990 after six years of service Shawn was discharged, and he enrolled as a civilian law enforcer. He lived in Nevada with his wife and daughter, Audrey. The marriage ended and Shawn had custody of Audrey. "She was my world," he said. "Strange because I never liked kids and didn't see myself with a family. But when I looked into newborn Audrey's eyes, a connection like none other was made. She is me, I am her." Although his future looked bright, he didn't like dealing with civilian social problems, which did not exist in the military. Police work was all he had ever done since he was seventeen. It was who he was. "I have been stabbed, sliced up, had teeth broken. My injuries were not too bad, only needed to get sewn up in the ER—in and out." It was really hard for him to handle the realization that he was not cut out for civilian police work. And having a young child to support increased the pressure. It was all downhill from there, and he spiraled into drug addiction and intermittent homelessness. He reached "the bottom of the cesspool," as he described it, running with some scary people. He knew he was going to end up dead or in prison.

Then Shawn got picked up for unpaid tickets, for not having his seat belt on, an expired registration, no front plate, a fictitious rear plate, and no insurance. In lieu of the fines, the judge gave Shawn five months in the county jail. He lost custody of Audrey. "Losing her cut deep. I failed her. I failed myself." This was hard on him, being under someone's control twenty-four/seven, not being able to do what he wanted when he wanted, but he was allowed to work in the county pound feeding the dogs and cleaning their cages. The dogs gave Shawn great comfort and really helped him. The jail was small and local and Shawn knew about half the prisoners, so no one messed with him. He decided then and there that he would never be locked up again.

After his stint in county jail, Shawn worked "one bullshit job after another." He was a good worker and someone his supervisors wanted to keep on as an employee, but little things would cause him to explode. He repeatedly got fired for his temper or because he would not show up for work. Sometimes he felt safer hiding in his apartment. "In 1996 I moved back to Ohio—thought I could quit drugs there. Didn't work out very well." He struggled with anger issues, hypervigilance, and anxiety. He was filled with hate and anger, for himself and the world. He understood that his temper was causing him to lose jobs, yet he continued to sabotage himself. Shawn knew something was wrong with him, and this time it wasn't drugs. A homeless veteran friend advised him to go to County Veterans Services for help. There Shawn finally sought counseling, and the VA gave his condition a name: post-traumatic stress disorder (PTSD), resulting from his time in the police force. With this diagnosis, Shawn could finally address it.

Shawn learned about medical marijuana, and although in 2006 doctors did not talk much about it for fear the US Drug Enforcement Administration (DEA) would pull their prescription licenses, he started using it. "Staying off drugs was not easy," he said. "The urge was still there and getting stronger. Cannabis helps addicts stay clean, helping you resist the urge to use drugs, up until the point that you no longer need them as a crutch." At his jobs, he decided to follow the rules to try to regain his honor. He did not use medical marijuana before or during work, but the metabolites stay in your system for weeks and the THC (tetrahydrocannabinol, the chemical responsible for most of marijuana's psychological effects) lingers for hours, so he did not take a permanent job over worries of a random drug test for employees. Things were not improving fast enough. He still had bad dreams, was still angry and bitter. "By 2011, I was at the end of my rope, worn down, tired. I decided that if 2012 was going to be the same, then it was time for me to exit."

IN JANUARY 2012, SHAWN FOUND A BOOK IN HIS LOCAL LIBRARY THAT offered possibility. *A Thru-Hiker's Heart: Tales of the Pacific Crest Trail* by Ray Echols was about thru-hiking the 2,600-mile Pacific Crest Trail (PCT), which Shawn had never heard of. "The author talked about the solitude of your mind and it sounded like something I should do." The book gave him hope there was another way, so he decided to hike the trail. In short order, he determined: "If I didn't get better on the PCT, I was going to eat a bullet." He read two more books, *The Pacific Crest Trail: A Hiker's Companion* by Karen Berger and Daniel R. Smith and Colin Fletcher's *The Complete Walker*—the bible for long-distance hikers, in print since 1968. Even though he was completely new to long-distance hiking, he put a plan in motion, auctioning off his belongings for money to hike the PCT. He bought all his hiking clothing at a thrift store and almost everything else at a discount store. The only things he paid full price for were hiking boots, a backpack, maps, and a bus ticket to San Diego.

Shawn hit the Pacific Crest Trail in April 2012 at the Mexico–California border. The entire hike cost him $500, counting food. He is mission-oriented. "When I start a thru-hike, I'll die before I don't finish." He learned by doing and by other thru-hikers sharing their knowledge along the way. Here is his story:

> I started the hike with the mindset that I would get better on the trail or die. Either way, the troubled mind will be stilled; it will be the end of suffering. I set out on a solo hike by choice but couldn't find the chance to be alone much, as there were so many hikers around. After a month, I was the same old asshole me. Then I began to be alone for a few days and there was no one to talk to. I started to spend more time in my head with my thoughts. I reviewed my past, thought about things people have told me. I always blamed my employers for my getting fired, for not getting along, but I began to realize that all the negative stuff I was going through was caused by me. I started to look at myself without the facade. People use facades—it is how we present ourselves to the world. This was not a pleasant thing, seeing myself for the first time without the facade. Guilt, shame, hurt, fear, and anger had

become all that I knew; it was all that I was. I thought, I had to deal with it, work it out on my own.

When some people hit this solitary, reflective stage on a thru-hike, they often quit. They don't like how they see themselves. But it was something you have to get through. A thru-hike is 20 percent physical and 80 percent mental. Only you can get you to the end. Hiking is a little more than walking, and walking ain't that hard. Once I had stripped away the illusions, I started to see lots of things differently. I began to see cause and effect and gained an understanding about myself. Most of the problems, I realized, were caused by me. Things began to gain more focus. "I act this way because of this incident that happened in my life." I started to feel calmer, more relaxed.

All of a sudden, on the trail, I woke up in my mind. I became more aware of everything. I noticed animal scat, and could smell a bear. I listened to the wind; I could hear hikers approaching.

Shawn remembers the exact spot where he woke up—Evolution Basin on the John Muir Trail section of the PCT.

I was sitting by himself, and all of a sudden, it was as if nature began speaking to me, in a barely audible, low female voice. I heard random words, as if I were being teased. Nature became real to me. I started to see the truth. Everything in nature is connected. We're on a giant ship floating in the universe. I share DNA with everyone. All are my cousins.

POSITIVE PSYCHOLOGY RESEARCHER CRAIG L. ANDERSON AND HIS GROUP at the University of California, San Francisco, studied a group of military veterans engaged in nature therapy. After the ecotherapy, the veterans felt that their general happiness, satisfaction with life, and social well-being had greatly improved, and their feelings of PTSD had greatly diminished.

The sense of awe that Shawn experienced has been studied for many years by psychologist Jennifer Stellar, PhD, at the University of Toronto. Stellar claims that this emotion plays a big role in our health, happiness, and well-being. Awe makes us feel small, in relation to something larger, so it humbles us and diminishes any feelings of entitlement, arrogance, and narcissism. A 2018 study by Stellar and her coauthor, Amie Gordon, PhD, found that experiencing awe also lowers levels of inflammatory cytokines and boosts the immune system.

"When I finished the PCT," Shawn said, "people could not believe I was the same person. . . . After four and a half months on the trail, I was more relaxed and happy. Before I began to hike, I was a pissed-off person. I dared you to try to knock the chip off my shoulder. Up until I hiked the PCT, I was a lying sack of shit. I made stuff up about my life. When you do that, after a while, your life becomes that lie. By stripping away that facade, you see your real self. After a thousand miles, all that extra bullshit started to slough off—it was weighty. Since hiking the trail, I'm more aware than ever." He made a major decision, to design his life around long-distance hiking because being in nature is where he feels the best. He hiked all summer long and worked in the winter so he could walk again come spring.

Around this time, Shawn heard of another veteran who was setting off to paddle the entire Mississippi River, in a solo canoe, to heal from her war-related trauma as a nurse. He had never even been in a canoe, but he was intrigued. "I was jazzed to do the river. I read a book about the history of the Mississippi that stretched back ten thousand years." In 2015, the two new friends started down the river in their canoes, staying together much of the time for company and support. Shawn found that paddling the Mississippi was not as hard as hiking. It was the first time in his life that he was serenaded by wolves at night. The number of bald eagles he saw on the river was astounding. He found a deep peace on the river, especially in northern Mississippi, which he loved the most. Doing without creature comforts was never hard for him. He is a minimalist. All his belongings in the world fit into two twenty-gallon waterproof totes and a backpack. "Makes moving by Greyhound easy," he claimed. "The only thing that mattered to me was what the river was doing for me and my mind."

Later that fall, Shawn realized that he was hungry for another experience in nature, so he hiked the Arizona Trail. While at the LF Ranch, Shawn did some trail maintenance for the owner, Maryann, and she offered him a job for when he completed his thru-hike. Shawn is a hard worker and is completely self-motivated. When he hit the Utah border on his hike, he turned around to come back to the ranch to work. Shawn was the first hired help Maryann had had in twenty years. She managed the ranch alone for forty years.

WHEN SHAWN WAS YOUNGER, AFTER HE GOT OUT OF THE MILITARY, HE ran fencing in Nevada and in many other states. He installed fences around schools, prisons, mines—split rail, wrought iron, and chain link. It is hard physical work, in all sorts of weather, but he liked it because it meant working outdoors and he was alone. After hiking the Pacific Crest Trail, he had worked for the US Forest Service on the Olympic Peninsula with the Washington Trails Association's backcountry crew. "Trail work and fence work are synonymous," he said. "You have to clear the terrain, get rid of brush, to make open spots to either put up a fence or create a trail."

When Shawn visited the LF Ranch as a hiker, the fence separating Maryann's cows from the wilderness area had been down for twenty years. The Forest Service had informed her that she needed to repair it ASAP. He knew nothing about ranching when he was hired, but Shawn did know fencing. He had always wanted to be a wrangler and work with a horse, and he wondered if now he would get the chance. Shawn was "on the fence" most of the year. He came back to the ranch headquarters about once a week to resupply. He cleared trail, cut new trail, built a line camp, ran pack horses to supply it, brought up four miles of fencing at a time, and then installed it. This lifestyle gave him tons of solo time. He put up four rows of barbed-wire fencing at the ranch. He built corrals that worked as traps for stock being moved around. "I loved 'the line,'" he said. "It's complete solitude. You don't hear anything man-made. This was my life. Just the wind, and the animals." Shawn had a lot of things to learn when he first arrived at LF Ranch. His horse, Buck, was difficult. But after a while, Buck and Shawn worked well together. "Buck is an awesome pack horse. I walk him everywhere. I got him to go anywhere and to carry anything."

Part of his job at the ranch was meeting and greeting the Arizona Trail thru-hikers and other guests. The ranch had a bunkroom for which Maryann charged a minimal fee. With prior arrangements, she cooked for hikers too. At the ranch they grew 70 percent of what they ate. Although the ranch was off-grid, there was an electrical outlet, that drew from solar panels, on the juniper tree outside the bunkhouse for charging. Shawn received room and board but no pay for his work.

As a ranch hand, sometimes his work could involve slaughtering, but Shawn told Maryann that he didn't kill unless he must. Shawn became very attached to the cattle. His job was to keep them calm to avoid weight loss, because when they are sold, they bring in more money if they are fit. If the cattle are accustomed to a human presence, they are less dangerous in the feed lot. They are born in the spring and rounded up in the fall, and in-between Shawn got to know their personalities. He felt like the piped piper, just leading them to slaughter, and that was hard on him. He believes that all life is sacred.

Shawn hadn't planned to stop hiking, but living at the ranch and working there gave him a great feeling. "I had forgotten what it felt like to belong. I didn't feel the urge to hike since I was living in the wilderness. I really enjoyed the ranch. It made me wonder if all the stuff I have been through was to help me see what is truly important in life." He now follows a Buddhist practice called the Eightfold Path that is designed to bring an end to life's suffering.

THE ROOSTERS WERE CROWING AT THE RANCH, AND A DOG CHASED A squawking peacock. The horses came in from the range for their evening meal of hay. A dust devil picked up and swirled around. The aluminum windmill creaked as it repositioned itself with a wind shift.

The screen door opened and slammed shut, and Shawn carried a pan of steaming, freshly baked muffins to a few white plastic chairs under the shade of a juniper tree. "I grew up in my grandmother's kitchen—Irish of course, and old-world cooking," he said to me. He loved making quick breads, muffins, applesauce cookies, and steamed carrot pudding. With a sun-weathered hand, he smoothed back his sun-bleached-blond hair. There were fine squint lines at the corners of his eyes. He held a cigarette in two fingers. It didn't much matter if it was lit or not; its presence helped him speak. His words were soft and smooth, the collective sounds of all that he had seen. You could listen to his stories all day.

The element of the Eightfold Path about caring for others is a wall that I have yet to break through. I know that I have a part of my soul missing. Sometimes I wonder if I ever had that part. What I do have is a huge hole in my life, where my daughter, Audrey, should be. I found a photo of me holding her as a baby and there was such serenity in my face.

When I moved to Seattle in the early 2000s, I thought Audrey and I would reconnect, but we couldn't seem to. It took my mom dying, in 2018, before we did get in touch. All of Audrey's life, all she heard was how bad a person I was. Except for Mom. She was always talking good about me, but never denied my addiction problems. When Mom was dying, Audrey was the one who let me know. From that point on, she and I started talking. I made her a promise that I would answer her questions with no sugar coating. Some questions I did not want to answer, but Audrey needed to hear the truth, no matter what it made me look like.

When I came to Seattle to see Mom before her death, Audrey and I really connected. Mom was able to see this. It was always her dream to see Audrey and me together. The day Mom died, Audrey phoned me. It was really hard on her. She had never seen any-one die and Mom had always been in her life. Funny, I was Mom's favorite kid and Audrey her favorite among the grandkids.

When Audrey needed me, I was glad to be near. We talk on the phone a lot now. She lives in Washington State. I want to be there for her. I have a lot of lost time to make up. I want to work and love Audrey.

This may sound weird, but I am glad it took so long to happen. Before I did the PCT in 2012, I wasn't the man I am now. Every time I won the fight with addiction, every mile I hiked, every day I spent in my mind, made me become someone again.

I have stepped so far outside of myself, and I have seen the pos-sibilities of where I can go as a human. I wasn't lost. I just forgot who I am.

CHAPTER 9

STEPHANIE CUTTS

US NAVY, 2002–2008

ACCORDING TO THE APPALACHIAN TRAIL Conservancy (ATC), of the thousands of hikers who start the Appalachian Trail at Springer Mountain in Georgia every year, hoping to walk the entire 2,180 miles, only one in four succeeds. The fact that five-foot, seven-inch, 250-pound Navy veteran Stephanie Cutts was one of those few hundred in 2013 might have surprised some observers. There are many reasons why hikers bail: injuries, blisters, sickness, accidents, family emergencies, or simply the trail being a lot harder to hike than imagined. The steep mountains in Georgia are hellacious. There are way too many when you are just starting out, carrying a loaded thirty-five- to forty-pound backpack that your body is not yet used to.

Todd and I had picked up Steph to offer some trail magic when she was coming through Pennsylvania. She wore a pretty pink sundress that she carried in her pack for "in-town" special occasions. Her colorful, full-sleeve tattoos appeared as if they were part of her dress. Around the campfire at our log home, she shared her story:

> I joined the Navy in 2002 when I was seventeen. I was a welder, a plumber, and a firefighter as part of Damage Control on the ship. As a team leader captain, I trained responders to react to any type of fire or toxic gas emergency, and I responded as well. My ship was deployed twice in the Persian Gulf and was based out

of Pearl Harbor. I was a rising star in the military, but while on deployment, I learned through a Red Cross message that Bill, my biological father, who did not raise me, had died. Because I was too far away to be flown off the ship to catch a flight home from Hawaii, I was the only member of my family who could not attend the funeral. His death affected me greatly.

I had unresolved childhood issues and always had these voices in my head telling me that I wasn't good enough for my father, that my life did not matter to him. I was always trying to prove myself to a man who didn't even bother to check whether I was alive. I used those voices to push myself, to be the best I could be, so one day I could throw it back in his face and say, "Look at everything I did. Look at who I became and I did it without you." I allowed my absent father to control my life, rather than live my life independently of him. When the words left my mom's lips on that phone call, "Bill died today," all I could say was "OK."

Those voices that pushed me were instantly gone. I felt lost without that inner motivation. I struggled to stay in shape, and the pounds began accumulating. I still did my job the best that I could, but I kept failing physical readiness weight standards. I would run every day at lunchtime but I was unable to make progress. The difference between my passing and failing the standards was literally a half inch on body measurements. Eventually, because I failed so many tests, I was released from my contract two years early. I was only able to serve six years instead of eight. After I got out of the service, I stopped trying and got progressively worse. I couldn't get off the couch. My top weight was 255.

My trauma in life probably began when I was seventeen. My mother went in for a checkup because she had stomach pains, discovered she had cancer in her right kidney, and had surgery right away. I could not understand how someone who believed so strongly in God could have this happen to her. That's when I stopped believing in God.

I hiked the Appalachian Trail to find God again, and for God to find me. I was also hiking to get my health back, get my life back. I wanted to find the motivation to put the rest of my grief and anger away. When I went down to Georgia and began the trail, I was so scared I was going to be in the worst shape of everyone. But everyone had a gut; no one was in shape! I was so excited to see those pot bellies! When it comes to hiking, I know my limitations; I go my own pace. On the trail, I continually reminded myself to not feel pressed to go someone else's speed. I wasn't worried anymore about my excessive weight.

It is very difficult to hike when you are heavy. It was hard to find hiking clothing that fits and didn't cause chafing. There are no plus-size items in proper hiking wear and I was a size 22–24 when I started the trail. I busted the crotch out of my pants, covered my terrible chafing sores with gauze pads and white surgical tape, and even tried duct tape, which was a terrible mistake. Finally, I found some bright blue pants with orange stripes at a Dollar Store that were trailworthy and comfortable. Even though I was still waddling with scabs on my inner thighs, I felt better. My feet and ankles were also swollen much of the entire hike, and I had to always sit with my feet propped up to let them drain.

THREE MONTHS LATER, WHEN STEPH REACHED THE TWO BOULDERS AT THE famous "Gateway," blocking her ascent up Mount Katahdin in Maine at the end of the trail, she shimmied through. "Yes!" she called out. "Two thousand miles ago and sixty pounds heavier, I could not have done this!"

For Steph, the Appalachian Trail was exactly what she needed. "A goal, something to believe in. I couldn't quit. Sometimes it wasn't very fun. I was hurting a lot. I know I am not a fast hiker, but I can do my two miles per hour. As time went on, I could tell how much good was happening to me. Once I got on track and had nowhere else to move but forward, I knew I would get there." Steph had not received her trauma from combat-related experiences, like many of the veterans profiled in this book, but through childhood trauma, which makes the brain more vulnerable to trauma in adulthood. The experiences she had while serving in the Navy compounded her trauma. It does not matter the source of the trauma, hiking the trail has the capacity to heal us all. It offers the gift of time away from the sorrows of the world and the space to think, accept, and forgive.

There was misty fog on the majestic monolith of Mount Katahdin when Steph arrived. The large wooden sign stating, "Springer Mountain, Georgia— 2,180 miles," emerged into view. Steph just cried and cried and hugged and hugged everyone with reckless abandon. There was no holding back her release of emotion. "I had finally silenced the voice in my head that told me I couldn't do something, that I wasn't good enough. These negative voices had plagued me since childhood and I worked on silencing them through-out my entire hike. I often thought about all the bad mistakes I made, and I learned to let go of them as the miles passed. The long distance—miles and months—gave me time to deal with it. Before my hike, I might have thought about stuff a day or two at a time, but then would lock it up and put it away for the year."

Psychologist Lynne Williams explains avoidance of painful thoughts this way: "It's the *avoidance* of facing, thinking about, feeling about, upsetting things from our life that keeps us stuck in unhealthy places emotionally. We distract ourselves from the memories, thoughts, and feelings with work, drugs, media, sex, etc. Long-distance hiking removes many of the distractions and impediments to facing our past."

The trail provided the space for Steph to heal. "The more I let myself heal," Steph continued, "the better I felt. The longer I did that, the lighter I felt. I was able to work through my issues and leave them at Mount Katahdin. The trail changed me back to who I used to be." Steph carried two small stones for the entire journey: one for her and one for her demons—a physical representation of the weight her soul had carried. That day on Mount Katahdin, she left those stones at the sign and walked away from her pain.

CHAPTER 10

ZACH ADAMSON

US ARMY RANGER, 2009–2013

*Heroes take journeys, confront dragons, and discover
the treasure of their true selves. Although they may feel
very alone during the quest, at its end their reward is a
sense of community: with themselves, with other people,
and with the earth. Every time we confront death-in-life,
we confront a dragon, and every time we choose life over
nonlife and move deeper into the ongoing discovery of who
we are, we vanquish the dragon; we bring new life to
ourselves and to our culture. We change the world.*
—Carol S. Pearson, *The Hero Within*

STEVE ADAMSON LEANED ON HIS son Zachary's hiking poles with every step. He leaned on his son's memory, for he needed Zach's help to get up the mountain. Steve swore he saw his son, swore he heard him in the woods, say, "You can do this, Dad." The four-mile climb up to Virginia's McAfee Knob on this Memorial Day weekend in 2014 was not just a physical challenge because of his two bad knees and the extra weight he carried; the emotional drain of the event was even greater.

Airborne Ranger Zachary Adamson (Appalachian Trail name "Shady") had become a 2,000-Miler on the trail the year before. He departed Springer Mountain, Georgia, only four months after returning home from Afghanistan at the conclusion of four years and five tours in Iraq and Afghanistan as a US Army Ranger. Zach got the idea to thru-hike the famous trail from his good friend and fellow Ranger, Eric Hario, who had planned to hike the entire trail once he got out of the military. Eric died on his first mission, so Zach carried Eric's dream forward and hiked for Eric and for himself. Three months after reaching the summit of Mount Katahdin in Maine, Zach died from a gunshot wound to the head. He was twenty-five years old.

The tragedy rocked the whole Appalachian Trail community as well as thousands of friends and family. The memorial climb up McAfee Knob was orchestrated by Travis Johnston, Zach's Machine Gun Team Leader who served with him in Afghanistan. A photograph shows Travis in the back of his pickup with his arm draped over the memorial stone he had created in Zach's honor. Travis's dull, sad eyes are like two dark stones, lifeless and empty. Veteran and author Doug Peacock evocatively described this look in his book *Walking It Off: A Veteran's Chronicle of War and Wilderness*. He writes, "Soldiers often return with death eyes; these may be the eyes of depression, to which all life looks dead, or the eyes of anger or withdrawal. The warrior has faced fear and an adversary too powerful. The soul flees."

Travis, a veteran of both Operation Iraqi Freedom and Operation Enduring Freedom, decided to thru-hike the AT to honor Zach, who had been one of his best friends. Together, they had experienced what Travis considered to be the worst day of his life. "Lying side by side in the prone position atop a ridge in Afghanistan, in the middle of a fire fight," Travis recalled, "I believe it to be the root of my struggle as well as his. That deployment has caused me to have the most trouble in my life, causing horrible recurring thoughts, and I know Zach felt the same." Zach had been a huge support to Travis in making him feel better about what happened that day. "It seemed as though we were both cornerstones in each other's lives, in which we could find peace and solace."

Travis remembered Zach as an amazing kid. "I couldn't have asked for a better AG [assistant gunner] or friend. On that deployment in Afghanistan, our company lost two amazing individuals, Staff Sergeant Jason S. Dahlke, twenty-nine, of Orlando, Florida, and Private First Class Eric W.

Hario, nineteen, of Monroe, Michigan, who was a good friend of Zach's and often spoke of hiking the AT." After Eric's death, all Zach talked about was thru-hiking the entire AT, both for himself and for his fallen Ranger brother. After completing the trail, Zach returned home to work with his family in Ohio. Both Travis and Zach's best friend, Sean Reilly, who was also in their platoon were unaware of how much Zach was struggling. "I didn't know how hard Zach took everything. Obviously, it was enough to cause him to leave this earth." Travis was in complete and utter disbelief when he heard the news. "Zach was the funniest, most lovable, charismatic, and genuine person anyone had ever met," he recalled. "He never met a stranger, and there wasn't a single person who did not like him."

Travis and Sean made their way to Ohio to help with the funeral. "It was there that I met Zach's trail family," Travis said. "I had known that the trail had made a very positive impact on Zach and his life, but it wasn't until I spoke with his friends that I realized just how influential the trail had been for him." It didn't take much thought before Travis knew that he had to thru-hike the AT in memory of Zach.

BUT PLANNING TO HIKE IN ZACH'S MEMORY WAS NOT ENOUGH. TRAVIS wanted to further commemorate Zach and find a way to provide some form of closure for himself as well as for Zach's family and friends. Zach had not been the first of Travis's platoon to take his life. Just months before, another member of their platoon, Sgt. Nate Boyden, had died by suicide. Travis decided to honor Zach on Memorial Day weekend of 2014. He started a GoFundMe campaign and raised more than $5,000 to create a large memorial stone and three small ones for each of Zach's family members. He flew Zach's family from Ohio to Virginia and paid for their food and lodging during their time there. All they had to do was show up at the airport. Travis orchestrated everything else.

The 150-pound memorial granite stone features two photos: one shows a serious Zach in full kit (field uniform with body armor, weapon, and ammunition), holding his M4; the second is a lighthearted, smiling Zach, the bearded thru-hiker. Travis arranged for Zach's family and friends to gather on top of McAfee Knob to celebrate Zach's life. This geological formation on Catawba Mountain in Virginia had been Zach's favorite spot on the entire Appalachian Trail because of its outstanding views. At an elevation of 3,197 feet, McAfee Knob has an almost 360-degree panoramic view of the surrounding Shenandoah Mountains and valleys.

On that Memorial Day weekend, Travis and Sean, as well as Zach's brother Jesse, carried the stone across the busy highway and placed it near the trailhead leading up McAfee Knob. Everyone in the group received a lit votive candle and filed over to the stone, spoke quietly to Zach, placed the candle there for him, and began to hike toward the summit. The walking stimulated many memories in those four ascending miles. Zach's father, Steve, told stories of taking the Adamson kids hiking and backpacking, of storms they got caught in, and fun times over the years. Stopping occasionally to sob and hug someone as they climbed, Steve showed photos of Zach on his phone. Nearly every highlight in his son's life was there for quick reference. More than any other place, Steve said, he feels Zach in the woods. He wants to return, time and again, to visit with his son. He said he needed more joy in his life. Steve and his wife, Rebecca, felt like in the four months since Zach's death, they had been drowning in their sorrow. In their grief, they both gained a lot of weight and were becoming reclusive.

Up on the mountaintop, Travis and Sean placed the stone in a perfect spot with the best view, and then laid out mementos of Zach on the rock: his knife, his medals, his hiking poles, and his photograph. A bottle of twelve-year-old Jameson Irish Whiskey, a favorite drink of Rangers, was passed around to pour into tiny plastic cups for a toast to Zach. Songs were sung accompanied by a guitar, and copies of the lyrics to the folksong "Wagon Wheel," a favorite of Zach's, were distributed so all could join in. The American flag was folded thirteen times into a tight triangle pillow with only the blue starred field showing, placed over Zach's mementos by a handful of hiking infantry combat veterans. Each family member, as well as Sean and Travis, took turns speaking about what Zach had meant to them, how they planned to go on with their lives, wanting to be more like Zach—embracing life, living large, and spending time in nature. Sean spoke of his memorable times with his best friend. Travis said how impressed he was that a few Rangers and Zach's hiking family from 2013 had come from states far and wide to pay their respects.

MANY IN THE MILITARY, ESPECIALLY A TIGHT GROUP LIKE THE RANGERS, believe that no one can be closer than their "Band of Brothers"—until they experience a thru-hike on the Appalachian Trail. To understand how their brotherhood can compare to a thru-hiking family, it's worth a look at who these men of the 75th Ranger Regiment are. Author Dick Couch in *Sua Sponte: The Forging of a Modern American Ranger* has examined the history of the Army Ranger dating back to colonial America. In the early 1800s these soldiers "ranged" the American wilderness, fighting American Indians as white settlers tried to take control of their land, when we were just a fledging nation. The Ranger wore leather moccasins and leggings, hung a small hatchet on his belt, slung a powder horn over his shoulder and carried a wool blanket, bread, salt pork, and his trusty musket. Today's Rangers look far different with their body armor of ballistic Kevlar plates, sixty pounds of gear including a machine gun with an infrared laser and a telescopic sight, but they were elite soldiers then as they are today.

The 75th Ranger Regiment is one of the most prestigious units in America's Special Operation Forces—a light-infantry force involved in direct-action missions. This combat assault team tracks down enemy fighters, captures or kills them, and disrupts insurgent operations. As Couch wrote: "The military in general and Rangers in particular are in the business of killing people." The 75th Ranger Regiment trains in all forms of airborne and mobile tactical operations, so they can arrive at the cutting edge of battle. Operating in small, tight-knit units, they are called in first, hence their motto: "Rangers Lead the Way!" Their male warrior bonding is unique and powerful—part fraternity, part family—and it is legendary. An Army Ranger covets his relationships with his fellow Rangers and holds them as high as any blood family member, if not higher.

Nothing can come close to that bond, or so a Ranger might think, until he sets foot on his long journey on the Appalachian Trail toward Maine. Zach Adamson, and then Travis Johnston one year later, were taken by surprise by the intense brotherhood that exists on the trail among long-distance hikers. When Zach's Memorial Day climb was staged, more than twenty hikers left their thru-hike at various points along the route and arranged to get themselves north to McAfee Knob. Although they were thru-hiking the year after Zach hiked, they had hiked with Travis and knew him well. They wanted to go to support him, and they showed up to help Travis heal.

Being part of a hiking/outdoor community helps replace the missing brotherhood, which so many returning vets experience. No longer having a close sense of community is one of the great losses when returning to civilian life. Many veterans find it challenging to replace or rebuild a strong network of healthy social connections. Sharing physical activities in nature, without the need to make oneself vulnerable emotionally, is a relatively easy way to work toward eventually being able to tolerate and develop more emotionally connected relationships.

THE SINGLE OVERWHELMING EMOTION ON THE MCAFEE KNOB MEMORIAL climb that day was an outpouring of love and support, for Zach as well as for friends and family in attendance. It is difficult for healing to occur in a safe home, behind closed doors and sturdy walls that have been constructed around one's heart, alone with demons and memories. Author and speaker Jim Rohn has said: "The walls we build around us to keep out the sadness, also keep out the love." On the descent from the mountaintop, Steve pondered aloud: "Maybe there are lives being saved here today." Perhaps he was referring to Zach's Ranger buddies, Travis and Sean.

Back at the trailhead, the sun's rays had grown low and were striking Zach's stone where it sat, the light from the flickering votive candles bringing his photographs to life. Travis sat by and spoke of that horrible day in Afghanistan, the day that became the worst nightmare in his and Zach's life. The experience still caused nightmares, torturing Travis with the question, "Should I have done it differently?" The firefight that haunted Zach until the day he died was not a typical Ranger mission, Travis said. "We did surgical shit in Iraq, clear out a house and take the target bad guys out. We had business to do and we were in and out before the sun came up. The fights in Afghanistan were different. We were clearing mountains and whole valleys sometimes, not just compounds or single houses. Some of those battles lasted twenty-four hours or more and consisted of heavy fighting and constant bombing."

There were other Ranger platoons fighting in those Afghan mountains during that particular firefight, Travis said. This mission was complex with a lot of moving pieces. Communication and orders from their platoon leader, who was not present, were confusing. Bad information had been disseminated. In the fog of war, Travis and his fellow Rangers were involved in what is called friendly fire, when firing from your own side causes accidental injury or death to your own forces. (also called "blue on blue"). Travis's platoon did not kill any fellow Americans in this particular mission, but life-altering injuries and unfathomable regrets did result. Travis had not yet forgiven himself. Perhaps walking the next seventeen hundred miles of the trail would allow him to work on that. Clinical psychologist Lynne Williams explained that what Travis was experiencing is "an example of 'dysfunctional guilt,' which creates the illusion that such horrible experiences are actually controllable. If he didn't have this belief, he'd be overwhelmed with the horrors that truly atrocious things are often *not* preventable."

STEVE AND REBECCA ADAMSON SHARED LETTERS FROM ZACH, HOPING TO give insight into what he had gone through. Excerpts from a letter he wrote after that horrible night in Afghanistan reveal that Zach was thinking about death and his own mortality.

Dear Momma and Daddy,

I feel such like a little boy! I love you two so much it's impossible to explain my feelings I have for you and the family. I can't even write this without tearing up. I just want you to know you really were the best parents that I could ever have! I don't know what I would do without you! I love you so, so, so much!

Today I said farewell to my friend! I feel so emotionally drained and it hurts even more when I think about his mom and dad and how they feel! He was only 19. . . . He was so young and had so much life ahead of him. . . . Wow, I know, it's war and people die but I always thought it was the guys that I saw or heard about, not my friend. . . . I'll never be the same after this!

We've only been in country for two weeks now and we already have many casualties and two KIA [killed in action] and we got over 200 EKIA [enemy killed in action]. This has been by far the most busy and craziest thing in my life. I've never seen so much and never knew my body could handle the shit I put it through!

There are a few things I must tell you now! Not to scare you but
it's a needed thing I must do just in case something does happen to
me! And at this point I know that anything could happen and that
just made me think that none of us are prepared to die. After last
night, I think most of us that went through that 26-hour mission
came back and wrote a letter to that special person or people just
in case, because that night in the KG Pass [Khost-Gardez Pass in
the Hindu Kush Mountains] was eye opening.

This is the most difficult fighting and different fighting that I
have ever seen. I'm so exhausted from fighting my way up mountains to the enemy shooting down at us with all kinds of firepower.
It's by far the scariest things I've went through but I know that
this is not the end of it. There is so much more fighting ahead! I'm
just scared of what's ahead in the future for me and my comrades.

Zach had made it safely home after four years of fighting, blind in one
eye from a training accident, partially deaf in one ear from an explosion
and heavy weapons, and suffering with traumatic brain injury. In a matter
of months, he transitioned from Ranger to thru-hiker on the Appalachian
Trail, where he received the gifts of peace, healing, and friendship. Returning home after war is often the most challenging part of military service.
Returning home from a six-month wilderness hike is also challenging. As
I wrote in *Journey on the Crest: Walking 2600 Miles from Canada to Mexico*: "Returning home is the most difficult part of long-distance hiking. You
have grown outside the puzzle and your piece no longer fits." It takes time,
patience, understanding from loved ones, and creativity to reinvent a new
life. Many veteran thru-hikers say the later experience can be almost as
traumatizing as the first. Zach had the heightened challenge of dealing with
both, pretty much back to back.

After summiting Mount Katahdin in October 2013 and returning home,
Zach wrote in his journal: "I'm stuck between a rock and a hard place. I'm
upset and depressed. I loved being on the trail, but I came back home thinking I could pick up where I left off, and I was obviously wrong. I don't know
what I want to do or where I want to go. What makes me happy is excitement,
adrenaline, new places, new adventures. Do I live the life that I feel has been
an amazing, once-in-a-lifetime opportunity; or live with family in Ohio, go

on weekend trips close by, have a house, get a girl, do what's 'normal'? I don't know." His struggles are evident, in hindsight. One of the "positive" realities of being part of a military mission in a war zone, or part of a thru-hiking community, is the intense sense of being alive every moment, in part resulting from the adrenaline rush, the heightened focus, constant scanning of the environment for danger, and the strong sense of meaning and purpose.

Returning to civilian life without a civilian career that has a strong sense of purpose—such as counselor, educator, or community responder—can leave returning veterans with little sense of meaning and purpose. In late October, Zach expressed similar thoughts in his journal:

> 12:35 a.m. When I try to sleep, my mind is racing about everything and anything. I feel like I forgot something so I check the locks on the door and my truck outside. I hear sounds that could be anything but I think it's someone breaking in. I feel my heart racing very fast to the point I feel like my heart might stop. I also hear ringing the loudest at night when everything is quiet. I also twitch at night—my entire body sometimes. I often lie awake and feel very scared, paranoid.
>
> 3:17 a.m. There's something wrong with me. I keep choking up and am about to cry. I yelled out loud, "What is wrong with me?!"

SADLY, WHAT MADE ZACH AN IDEAL CANDIDATE FOR MOLDING INTO A WARrior made him equally prone for post-traumatic stress after experiencing that trauma. "Everyone who experiences combat comes back with PTSD," writes author Dave Grossman in his book *On Killing: The Psychological Cost of Learning to Kill in War and Society*. "The only question is to what extent their mind and psyche are damaged and how they cope with it." Eighteen- and nineteen-year-old males are the ideal candidate for the military, no matter the branch. Erik Steele, who wrote "How the 19-Year-Old Brain Can Both Awe and Appall Us" for the *Bangor Daily News*, explains that the brain was designed by evolution for purpose without much perspective, passion without much reason, reproduction without much responsibility, and performance without caution, just the right time in a young man's life to convince him to go off to war to kill, but especially traumatizing afterward.

In the book *Cognitive Processing Therapy (CPT) for PTSD*, author Patricia Resick, professor of psychiatry and behavioral sciences at Duke University, explores neurobiology and PTSD. "Neurobiology helps us to understand why younger people are more likely to develop PTSD," she writes. "The prefrontal cortex is not fully developed until humans are well into their twenties, so not only are young people likely to be traumatized, but they have fewer resources to deal with trauma once it occurs. When trauma occurs in a brain that is not fully formed, significant and persistent changes to neural tissue integrity can occur in certain regions of the brain. Some of those changes meant that brain networks were permanently altered, which could inhibit recovery." When we are young, Dr. Resick explains, we tend to practice binary thinking, in limiting terms of right or wrong, good or evil; but as we grow older and have more life experiences and have seen "bad things happen to good people," our older, more sophisticated brains have more places to put trauma. We are more likely not to experience long-term, post-traumatic stress.

STEVE AND REBECCA ALSO SHARED A LETTER TO ZACH FROM THRU-HIKER "Patches," who hiked with Zach and had been unable to attend the funeral. Her words provide insight into how Zach (a.k.a. Shady) was sometimes still haunted, even on the trail. Despite his torment, however, he tried to protect his trail family.

> At first glance, Shady was just a thru-hiker like the rest of us, a part of our community, a part of my trail family. As thru-hikers we know, "You can leave the trail, but the trail never leaves you," and as a vet, Shady had left the war, but the war hadn't left him. Hiking with him during the day you wouldn't know he'd been an Airborne Ranger in the US Army and that he had served one tour in Iraq and three tours in Afghanistan. He was part of our crew. He tried to take care of us and we tried to take care of him.
>
> Shady's war memories stalked him on the trail and ambushed him in his sleep. At night, he tried to protect us from foes we couldn't see and only he could know. When a sharp screech pierced the quiet night in Maine's 100 Mile Wilderness, Shady

threw himself over the person next to him in the shelter to protect him with his body. He thought that an improvised explosive
device (IED) was going off, and he was going to save as many of
us from it as he could. He didn't hesitate. He didn't think about
what would happen to him; he just did what he could to protect
us. None of us had any doubt that Shady was willing to sacrifice
himself to protect us. It did not matter that what he was actually
protecting us from was an alarm clock going off in his pack. We
loved Shady. I wish that we could have protected him the way he
tried to protect us.

THE MCAFEE KNOB MEMORIAL CLIMB THAT TRAVIS ORGANIZED IN MEMORY
of Zach created many positive ripples, just like Zach's life had touched so
many other lives. With the exquisite surrounding backdrop, McAfee Knob
towering tall with clouds beyond, it felt like heaven was right there. Travis
shared his final thoughts with those gathered: "Zach did not practice the
trail concept of 'Leave No Trace,' for everywhere he went he left his residual
love and huge spirit. Hiking the AT was Zach's first five million steps toward
recovery. It didn't fix him, but it helped. He just needed more."

PART THREE

THE TRAIL
HEALS

CHAPTER 11

TRAVIS JOHNSTON

US ARMY RANGER, 2006–2010

Before I can tell my life what I want to do with it, I must
first listen to my life telling me who I am.
—Parker J. Palmer, *Let Your Life Speak:*
Listening for the Voice of Vocation

"AT THE TIME THAT ZACH died, I was a very sick individual," Travis Johnston said, recalling his Ranger buddy Zach Adamson, whom he had fought alongside in Afghanistan. "I was physically and emotionally irresponsible on every level. I was functioning, but I was dead inside. At the funeral, I was in disbelief. Zach had been right by my side on the worst day of my life. He was feeding me rounds. We were in it together. I had always felt a sense of duty to him, being his Team Leader."

Zach took his own life in 2013, and Travis never heard his cry for help. He hadn't spoken to Zach in several months and had no idea he was suffering, so Travis was struggling with guilt. Simultaneously, Travis was struggling for his own survival as well. The life of an Army Ranger is foreign to civilians and, to a great extent, even to those who serve in other military branches. "Army Rangers train to be aggressive; it's our job in the Seventy-fifth Ranger

Regiment," Travis said. "Every six months we were deployed. Rangers crave jumping out of airplanes at night with a machine gun strapped to them onto an airfield that's occupied by the enemy. You are trained to move *toward* the sound of gunfire, not away. You go there to kill. You are trained to kill and you *want* to. It's a point of pride to be a part of something so elite and so extreme, doing the things that no one else wants to or simply cannot do. It goes against all human nature. Your lines of normality and what is reasonable are blurred from day one."

As Travis explained it:

> When you're not deployed, you still want to do crazy shit. It's in your blood. While off-duty, I either took part in or witnessed other Rangers drinking and driving, binging until we'd vomit, wrecking vehicles, fist fighting, and sleeping with women indiscriminately. It seemed normal. A running joke between us was to run away as the police would respond to one of our fights and scream, 'Semper Fi!' to throw them off, as if we were Marines. I doubt it ever worked, but it was funny. Everything we did was funny. There was no line unless you got caught. We'd piss on bar tops, set guys on fire, shoot pistols in the air from our open truck windows. By no means was this what everyone did, but to say it was common is fair. Risky and outrageous behavior was accepted and in some ways, expected. There is a Ranger saying that is printed on T-shirts: RUN-GUN-DRINK-FUCK-FIGHT, which sums up the mentality pretty accurately. The culture revolves around being extreme. It hinges on individuals being able to step up in an unnatural way. It was so reckless, and in the end, it cost me and many other Rangers.

THE PSYCHE OF A RANGER IS UNIQUE INDEED. TRAVIS DESCRIBED A WAY of life that few can imagine, but what happens when the mission is over? "We lived like this when we weren't on missions because in some way, we needed to match that high level of stimulation that we were constantly receiving," he said. "It was a fun, relaxed day when we got to put on a parachute and jump into water out of the back of a Chinook helicopter. That level of constant stimulation, drive, and adrenaline is overwhelming. When you stop, you crave it. It's more than a lifestyle and a job; its addictive, like a drug. I am not saying that every Ranger felt this way or behaved in this manner, but it was common, and I was a part of it."

Travis sought professional help in 2010 at the end of his time in the 75th Ranger Regiment. His career had suffered and begun to unravel. After treatment, he was sober for two years, but eventually he began to drink again, more and more, until Zach's death.

THE SUICIDE RATE FOR ACTIVE-DUTY US MILITARY MEMBERS IN 2019 WAS the highest on record since the US Department of Defense began tracking self-inflicted deaths in 2001. Since the beginning of the wars in Afghanistan in 2001 and Iraq in 2003, military suicides have so increased across the board that they have outpaced combat deaths. Special Forces Operations have the highest numbers. "Constant deployments and unrealistic mission expectations are taking their toll on these elite forces," said top commander Army General Raymond Thomas of Special Operations Command. David Joslin, US Army captain, medic, and founder of the veterans' organization Remedy Alpine, which uses adventures in nature to heal wounded veterans, has studied the issue of suicide in the military. "To better understand why Warriors and Veterans appear to so readily contemplate and complete suicide," Joslin points to three factors that seem to make suicide an acceptable alternative for warriors and veterans:

> First, from the moment we join the military service we are taught that we are expendable, we are merely government property, and our own life is institutionally devalued. Second, as we train and prepare for war, we are taught to accept our own death—we save the final round for ourself as an alternative to capture, we engage and deploy on missions with no viable outcome other than death: "suicide missions." Third, we are trained to very efficiently and effectively deliver death—the ultimate job of a Warrior is to kill. And in this, human life in general is devalued. In considering these three factors of conditioning, why is anyone surprised that Warriors and Veterans consider suicide as a viable alternative when they are at their darkest and lowest place?

TRAVIS WAS CERTAINLY IN A DARK PLACE AT ZACH'S FUNERAL IN OHIO, BUT something struck him that gave him a bit of hope. "I wondered who all these fuckin' trail hiking hippies were that came to remember Zach." A number of thru-hikers from Zach's journey on the Appalachian Trail the previous year had made the trip to honor Zach. "I thought, 'They don't know my brother.' But they were such happy people and something about them spoke to me through my depression, and I thought, 'I want to be happy too.'" When he saw Zach's casket, Travis came to the realization that this could be him real soon too. "Dead or in prison—that was where I was headed and I didn't want either. At the funeral, I was forced to look at my own life. Zach's death left a large hole in me, but it also woke me up." Travis explained that many Rangers experience a slow and steady decline when they get out of the military. "They either crash and burn or something wakes them the fuck up. I knew that I had to move fast or I, too, would probably soon be in a casket."

Travis decided to plan a thru-hike along the Appalachian Trail that would include a memorial for Zach at McAfee Knob, elevation 3,197 feet, on Catawba Mountain in Catawba, Virginia. "Before Zach's death," he recalled, "I would have never believed I would hike a trail like the AT, nor would I have wanted to. Hiking felt and looked like a waste of time to me."

When Travis began hiking the AT for Zach in 2014, he took all the meds that the VA prescribed for him—all nine of them. About two months into his hike, his prescriptions ran out and he crashed. He found himself hiking alone, apart from his trail friends, which forced him to look at the demons inside. "It was easy to keep them hidden when I was with other folks. When I found myself alone, I lived in a dangerous place inside my head. I hated hiking by myself. I couldn't get past certain things." He grew very depressed. Nightmares returned. He would dream he was in a firefight and did not have his weapon; he'd be jumping out of an airplane and not have his helmet. "It was the closest I came on the trail to saying, 'Fuck this,' and calling it quits."

Then Travis had a dream where Zach appeared and spoke to him. They were having a conversation about whether or not Travis should complete the trail. Zach told him, "You need to know what it's like [to finish]." That dream gave Travis the kick in the butt that he needed. He decided that he could not quit, and he must complete the trail. After the dream, every day got consistently and exponentially better. Every step north toward Mount

Katahdin brought more healing. The memorial climb had given Travis a mission, and the ceremony offered closure, but it also made clear that this hike was a last-ditch attempt to save himself from going down that same dark road. "On McAfee Knob," Travis said, "the pain from Zach's death reverberated through everyone present, and it became clear how much *I* meant to others. I realized that I was worth saving too. I had a responsibility to not just exist, but to really live and be healthy, too."

AFTER THE MEMORIAL CLIMB FOR ZACH, TRAVIS BEGAN HIKING FOR HIM-self, to save his own life. Over the miles, the trail provided precious gifts like a massive amount of time to reflect, for the trail removes distractions. In nature, he could separate and distance himself from his past. He learned that he was not in control of what happened in the war, or the weather on the trail, for example, yet he *is* in control of his thoughts and his future. Travis began to examine his life, the relationships he had with others, and put thought into a future occupation. He made a plan of what he wanted to fix about himself. A clear-cut symptom of PTSD is feeling out of control, with the inability to achieve goals. Gifting himself the time to walk a long-distance trail allowed him the space and time to examine these things about himself, however uncomfortable, even painful. As he recalled:

> Hiking from Georgia to Maine gave me a new mission and my trail family became my new brotherhood. I learned that being completely isolated is not good for me. I need a family who is experiencing the same hardships and joys as I am, just like in the military. I also learned that I had to be patient and accept this new experience, replace those bad memories with new good ones. War is not normal but being in the woods and hiking the trail felt nor-mal, it felt good, and it wasn't a masking agent like drugs or alco-hol. Looking back now, I had been so close to dying many times. I am 100 percent sure I would have ended up like Zach if I kept on course. When I descended off Mount Katahdin in Maine, I didn't feel like I had just finished the AT; I felt like I was starting the rest of my life. Moving forward, anything was possible.

HIKING THE APPALACHIAN TRAIL WAS TRAVIS'S LAUNCHING PAD TO BECOM-
ing a healthier person and living a richer, more fulfilling life. He is no longer
focused on numbing his feelings or memories, but on facing and working
through them. "It was as if I needed some sort of major rocket power, a mass
explosion, to help break through gravity and launch me away from Earth
and my old unhealthy way of living and thinking." He made a five-year plan
to earn the Triple Crown of hiking: completing the Appalachian Trail, the
Pacific Crest Trail, and the Continental Divide Trail. He longed to explore
the world and so began to travel, approaching it with curiosity—learning
about world history, sampling different foods, and meeting fascinating
people. He crossed off many countries, continents, and experiences on his
bucket list.

World travel emboldened Travis, as he was finally experiencing *healthy*
risk. When encountering strangers, he would ask himself, "What would
Zach do?" Always friendly, warm, and forthcoming, Zach lit up an entire
room when he entered. And similarly, Travis extended himself and talked to
everyone. He told Zach's story, said he was traveling in Zach's memory and
hence kept him alive as he spread Zach's magic around the world. Travis was
finally distancing himself from the Rangers and the Ranger culture. He began
to cultivate a new identity. He was finding a new purpose, a new normal.

IF TRAVIS HIKED THE APPALACHIAN TRAIL FOR ZACH, HE HIKED THE PACIFIC
Crest Trail in 2016 as a gift to himself, celebrating his last year in his
twenties. Zach had planned to hike the PCT after the AT. While on that
trek, Travis had another epiphany. He could no longer live his life asking
himself, "What would Zach do?" At twenty-nine, he was older than the
twenty-four-year-old Zach had been when he died. If Zach were here,
Travis knew, he would certainly have made changes as a result of his own
personal growth. Travis himself should be growing as well, while keeping
Zach's memory close. He thru-hiked the PCT with a different mindset
and mission than he'd had on the AT. This time, he wanted to learn more
about himself, practice forward-thinking, further his own healing, and
take control of his life.

Travis approached the trail with full freedom and open-mindedness.
He did not plan to get involved romantically, but on the PCT in Southern

California he met Kaya, another thru-hiker. "Kaya is so sweet," he said. "She helped me set new goals: become a kinder person, and be as honest as I can. I used to be a real shitty person when it came to women and my romantic relationships. It's not something I'm proud of. Now, when I behave poorly, Kaya immediately corrects me and I reply, 'Roger that,' and I do my best to change. Kaya is my sounding board. If I'm in the gutter or going off the rails, she lets me know." Travis seemed to deal with all the death, loss, and guilt connected to the wars by having limited, unhealthy relationships with women, where he felt in control. He might say he was more likely to focus on *his* feelings, wants, and needs. Meeting Kaya taught him healthier ways of interacting intimately that incorporated the 'brotherhood' behaviors from the military. When you have each other's backs, you are *not* focused on your own wants and needs. You are making loving sacrifices for the greater good of your beloved, be they your military buddies or your life partner.

Travis learned peacetime living skills on the trail. In a war zone, you have to quickly learn to overlook things that will never represent danger, and instead focus on potentially dangerous things. On the trail, he learned to truly see the beauty in flowers, cloud formations, and faraway vistas. He learned to focus on wonder and creativity. While that type of focus would have gotten him and/or his men killed in a war zone, he learned to be present in the immediate moment in nature, to use all of his senses and to experience the sensations of calm, awe, and innocence.

Travis and Kaya made the decision to spend their winters in exotic locations, working as dive instructors and managing dive shops. This winter lifestyle provides them with peace and meditative time in the beautiful underwater world, so it is a perfect mix. Although the dive experience is short-lived, only an hour or so, compared with a months-long thru-hike, its healing benefits are huge. They thru-hiked the Continental Divide Trail in 2019, just for the sheer joy of it, which also gave Travis the coveted Triple Crown Hiker status. Accomplishing this massive goal is just what an Army Ranger needs: focused direction and carrying out a mission.

"HIKING IS HEALING," TRAVIS BELIEVES. TO DATE, IN ADDITION TO THE Triple Crown, he has hiked Spain's Camino de Santiago del Norte (500 miles), the 200-mile Scottish Highland Trail, England's Pennine Way, and Peru's Salkantay Trail. There are many more long trails on Travis and Kaya's horizon. The trails have helped Travis walk toward peace. Studies show that spending time in forests and in green natural areas actually leads to a happier, more fulfilled life. These magical places significantly lower your body's concentration of cortisol, as well as your pulse, your blood pressure, your sympathetic nerve activity (the flight-or-fight response) while increasing your parasympathetic nerve activity (rest and digest response).

The Japanese have known this for decades. Groundbreaking research begun in 1982 by the Japanese Ministry of Agriculture, Forestry, and Fisheries resulted in the term *shinrin-yoku*, meaning "taking in the forest atmosphere," or "forest bathing." The ministry studied the effects of merely sitting passively in a natural environment in twenty-five forests across the country. The study originated as an effort to promote public health as well as forest conservation. Since then, twenty thousand "forest bathers" have been documented showing significant improvement in their physical and emotional health. A minimum of two hours a week shows a significant improvement. Just think how much happiness, peace, and positive change a long-distance hike across the nation's wildest mountains can create? Travis knows the answer:

> The trails were a kind of beautiful bridge in my life. They helped me see things more clearly, for hiking strips away everything that doesn't matter. The trails helped me grow and set me up for the long term. Before, I could not believe that I even had a future. I simply could not envision one. I never thought that I would live this long, or even want to. Who I am today is very far from that Ranger who just arrived home from deployment.
>
> It has taken so long to arrive here. I have taken so many steps. It's even hard for me to identify with that stage in my life. I rarely talk about being in the Army and only when people ask. I'm glad to have had the experience of being a Ranger. It's important to me and I wouldn't give it up, but now it is only part of my identity. It's just part of my journey to whom I have become.
>
> Today, I feel so much better. I no longer live so recklessly and take unnecessary risks just for the hell of it. I have a future that

I think about and it influences my decisions. Now, I just have to figure out the best way to give back and help my fellow veterans achieve what the natural world, world travel, and the trails have given me.

CHAPTER 12

SEAN REILLY

US ARMY RANGER, 2010–2015

*This time there are no tears. This time, there is only
emptiness and I feel it set in the straight line of my mouth.
I am not strong enough for this. I want an earthquake, a
hurricane, anything . . . even the devil . . . to rush out and
stomp on me, break me into little pieces and hurl me to the
stars, let me go back with those people I love. Please.*
—Kathleen DeMarco

ARMY RANGER SEAN REILLY WAS watching how the trail in the southern Appalachians was transforming his buddy Travis Johnston. Travis had
never seen anything like the variety and sheer number of beautiful wildflowers that burst forth in the southern mountains every spring, and his
Facebook page was littered with his close-ups of the delicate flora. Hiking
had provided a lens onto their fragile world. Sean imagined his muscled,
tattoo-covered Ranger buddy with his chiseled jaw and intense eyes on his
hands and knees in the dirt waiting for the wind to stop and the sun to hit the
petals just right, so he could capture his shot. The distance between being
hypervigilant and looking for danger, Sean's current reality, to ignoring all
stimulus and focusing on the ground to photograph flowers was enormous.

Sean joined Travis on the Appalachian Trail in the Great Smoky Mountains of Tennessee for a total of six weeks. "Right away," he said, "I noticed a difference in Travis's eyes. They twinkled with joy." Sean had seen Travis after the death of their good friend, Zach Adamson. These eyes were a far cry from how they looked then, before he began his thru-hike. But on Charlies Bunion, where the landscape was exposed and craggy, Sean was brought right back to Afghanistan's Hindu Kush Mountains and the day of the platoon's horrific firefight. In Sean's mind, in his body memories, the scene looked remarkably like the terrain around the Khost-Gardez Pass (the K-G Pass), a high mountain pass at an elevation of 9,413 feet. The First Battalion Rangers had been sent in to disrupt the insurgents' training camps, where they found tents packed with ammunition. Sitting atop Charlies Bunion in the Smokies, surveying the surrounding rugged mountains, Sean swore he heard a couple of rounds go off.

"You need to replace those bad memories with newer, happier memories," Travis told him. Sean had recently returned home from his last deployment in the Middle East and still sported a military haircut and was clean-shaven. Travis had been out of the military for a few years and already had several hundred miles of hiking on his boots. His rust-colored beard was an admirable length for a thru-hiker, and his eyes danced with merriment. Sean wanted some of what Travis had. He longed to clear out the destructive voices in his head and replace them with the sound of the wind, birdsong, and spring peepers. The time since he'd left his Ranger battalion had been the loneliest, most difficult time in his life.

INSTEAD OF THRU-HIKING LIKE TRAVIS HAD, SEAN TOOK A DIFFERENT TACK. He traveled to Abu Dhabi in the Persian Gulf, where we worked as a contractor for the United Arab Emirates (UAE) military, teaching their medics first aid. Sean experienced a different side of Muslim culture, since the UAE is extremely westernized even though many wear head wraps. "Living in Abu Dhabi increased my self-confidence to live peacefully in a Muslim environment with the people and the culture," he said, "but I didn't have my Ranger buddy support system over there. When I heard the Muslim call to prayer, it continued to be a trigger, even after a year in-country, as well as when I saw a hijab." Indeed, during some combat training drills with

US military, the Muslim call to prayer is played over the loudspeakers to better simulate where the soldiers would be fighting and to increase their anger response. This planted a psychological association between combat and the prayer, further dehumanizing the enemy, which is done to get the soldier to kill and increase his own chances of staying alive.

"Humans have natural inhibitions about killing," author and psychologist Dave Grossman explains in his book *On Killing: The Psychological Cost of Learning to Kill in War and Society*. According to Grossman, "We have become good at training people to kill as a reflex and creating cold-blooded killers. The key to this is conditioning through desensitization of the humanity of the enemy." A "hadji" (derogatory slang used by troops in Iraq to describe an Iraqi Muslim citizen) is easier to kill than a father or a son. Grossman coined the term "killology"—the study of the psychological and physiological effects of killing and combat on the human psyche—and studied the factors that enable and restrain a combatant's killing of others. Retraining your brain and changing back is hugely challenging.

After they separated from the Army, both Travis and Sean accepted good-paying jobs working for the UAE military as first-aid instructors. Although Travis returned stateside after their initial contract was fulfilled, Sean decided to stay on since he had met a Canadian woman working in Abu Dhabi and fell in love. Remaining in the UAE for an extended period of time, however, was very difficult psychologically for Sean, and his PTSD grew worse. He experienced night terrors, anxiety, and anger throughout his day. He found himself drinking a lot. The drugs issued to him through the VA made him feel lethargic and groggy. He made frightening posts on Facebook, like typing on Zach's memorial page saying that he would see him soon. "I don't want to hold this in," he wrote. "I feel the darkness killing me. I feel these demons that I try to drown grabbing at my neck. I see a dark figure in my dreams call to me to the dark depths of a cold, endless doorway." It happened on anniversaries—of Zach's death, on Zach's birthday, of significant Ranger events. Photos popping up on Facebook of past memories were dangerous triggers for Sean of unresolved grief, and the depression would come in large waves. "I cry in my dreams and it hurts more when I wake up," he said. "I miss him so much."

Sean longed to be with his best friend. His grief led to torment. Scholar Michael Norman has written about this in his book *These Good Men:*

Friendships Forged from War. "I know why men who have been to war yearn to reunite," Norman explains. "Not to tell stories or look at old pictures. Not to laugh or weep . . . they long to be with the men who once acted their best . . . men who sacrificed and suffered . . . who were stripped raw . . . right down to their humanity." It comes down to a common fate, he says. "I did not pick these men. They were delivered by fate and the military. But I know them in a way I know no other men. I have never given anyone such trust. They were willing to guard something more precious than my life. They would have carried my reputation—the memory of me. It was part of the bargain we all made, the reason we were all so willing to die for one another."

Why had Zach not reached out to Sean when he was suffering and let him talk him off the ledge like he had done before when he was depressed and drunk? Why did he leave his best friend behind? Why couldn't Sean have done something to save him? Part of the Ranger creed that all Rangers memorize and recite has to do with never leaving a Ranger buddy behind. "I will never leave a fallen comrade to fall into the hands of the enemy." A suffering surviving Ranger might take that creed to include the "enemy" PTSD. Although Zach was ultimately responsible for his own life, Sean argued that it was also his responsibility to rescue Zach.

Dr. Patricia Resick, an expert in cognitive processing therapy, explains it like this: In bootcamp your sense of being an individual is stripped away and you are built up as part of a unit. Take that unit away, take that buddy away, and you experience tremendous loss. The soldier has to tell himself new messages however, for the only person who can truly prevent a suicide is the one who wants to do it, and if he really does want to, it is impossible to stop. The loved one left behind thinks there must have been something he could have done to prevent it and hangs on to the false belief that he had control when the situation was completely out of his control. If he feels guilty and blames himself, he doesn't have to face that awful reality that much of life *is* outside your control. The anger Sean felt toward Zach and in life in general has to do with accepting the really awful reality that loved ones can get hurt and die, and you can't do a thing about it.

In response to Sean's scary Facebook comments, his Ranger buddy Travis would often reach out with concern. "Sean needs help," Travis said, and thought the trail would be good for him, help him sort out his emotions and thoughts. "I cry about Zach whenever I need to," Travis said. "Sean has not cried yet. He needs to mourn and needs time in the woods to do it." According to neuroscientist William H. Frey II, author of *Crying: The Mystery of Tears*, who has spent more than twenty years studying crying and tears, emotional crying is not a sign of weakness but a very healthy thing for our bodies. Tears act as a safety valve releasing excess stress hormones and toxins that build up when stress levels reach an all-time high. Tears signal the release of feel-good hormones like oxytocin and endorphins as well as activate the parasympathetic nervous system and restore the body to a sense of balance. When chronically elevated levels of stress hormones remain in the body, physical ailments can occur.

Sean's girlfriend Carly, now his wife, was right by his side in the UAE. Yet he did not disturb her with his grief. Clinical psychologist Lynne Williams, who has worked with PTSD among veterans in her clinical private practice and in the prison system, says that one of the ways to cope with the grief and loss when a veteran buddy dies by suicide or is killed in action is to distance oneself from other people. To protect himself from the overwhelming emotions of loss and grieving and to keep his pain at bay, Sean avoided any kind of close, intimate contact. Healthy people, like Carly, express the normal range of human emotions the PTSD sufferer doesn't know how to handle. Unfortunately, the only way *through* grief is to talk, share memories, express emotions, tell about sad or scary parts, open up about the loneliness, the guilt, the stuff we meant to say or do with someone but never got around to. It is impossible to grieve without feeling intense emotions, and being emotionally numb keeps one stuck with unresolved grief. Sean needed to learn to share with Carly.

Sean was in the UAE for sixteen months. "Here in Abu Dhabi, everything became clear to me," he realized. "My issues, my pain, my suffering. I had grown tired of this constant internal struggle to feel sane. I had grown tired of watching me destroy myself. I had grown tired of looking for the enemy. I was exhausting myself trying to behave like a Ranger. I was no longer in the military fighting bad people. I know the first step in getting better is admitting that I have a problem." In the spring of 2016, he decided to gift himself a thru-hike, too. Travis had finally convinced him that he needed it, too. "I'm ready for the healing of the AT."

ON MARCH 21, 2016, ZACH'S BIRTHDAY AND TRAVIS'S APPALACHIAN TRAIL departure date, Sean set off from Springer Mountain, Georgia, to begin his own thru-hike, with Travis sending him off, of course. Sean carried Zach's dog tags and the shell from the bullet that killed him as he carried his memory north. After Travis left the trail, the reality of what Sean was undertaking sank in—there was nowhere for him to hide from his thoughts. There was no hard liquor to anesthetize him. "The trail is breaking him down a bit and making him question things," Travis said. "Sean is right where I was at this point. It is a hard thing. I needed it and so does he." One night in the Smokies, early in his journey, Sean was lying in his tent and saw another hiker's campfire glowing through his nylon walls. It brought back bad memories of burning bodies—he had to pack up and hike into the night to get away.

Sean's sister Ashley wrote a poem about his time on the trail and how it might save him:

> *"Sunshine Sean-bob"*
> *Stick deadly hands,*
> *now loosened.*
> *Gripping the trekking poles with determination.*
> *Heel-toe, heel-toe,*
> *a rhythm drilled deep into a deadpan mind.*
> *Blistering soles flexing into the bouldered path,*
> *that are secured in durable boots.*
> *Similar to the pair that once marched in uniform,*
> *but now are neglected.*
> *The blissful light through the trees,*
> *highlighting the streaming beads of sweat,*
> *sinking into the roughness of your beard.*
> *A new disguise, same brave face.*
> *Formally smooth and clean,*
> *perpendicular to high and tight.*
> *Stillness of the night drifts you off to sleep,*
> *under the moon and stars.*
> *Frogs croaking a symphony,*
> *tree leaves rustling in unison.*

Overpowering chaotic night terrors of the past.
Mile by mile,
your knees grow stronger,
the mind becomes purer.
Seeking peace and serenity,
a new perception of life.
Following a new path
traveled by many.
Taking in the wondrous beauty,
dragged out for miles and miles.
A reminder that the civilian life is colorful,
not blank and dark.
So don't give up,
not on this life,
because it won't give up on you.
Even if it takes 2,168.1 miles, 7 months.
You can do it, you have to do it.
Because I want my brother back.

AS THE HUNDREDS OF MILES TICKED AWAY BEHIND HIM, SEAN'S NIGHT TER-
rors gradually decreased. He began to see butterflies as messages from the
other side, which he interpreted as Zach's spirit taking on that form. As he
recalled a particular memory of Zach, a butterfly would flit by. In Sean's
entire thru-hike, he probably experienced sixty butterfly "visits."

When Sean reached McAfee's Knob in Virginia, eight hundred miles
later, he relived Zach's memorial hike the year before in his mind and realized he had reached an important milestone in his own healing. On this
second time around on McAfee's Knob, the anger Sean previously felt
toward Zach's suicide had dissipated. The trail was working its magic on
him. Sean spent a full-moon night atop the knob with Zach. He laid out his
Army Ranger military challenge coin, which symbolizes unit identity and
brotherhood, and Zach's photo on the rocks and waited for the sun to rise.
The moment the sun rose, a butterfly flitted by. Before his thru-hike, the
only way Sean had known how to think about his best friend and mourn
his death was through drinking heavily, which is a very big part of Ranger

culture. Now he was celebrating Zach's life and their friendship out in the healing lap of nature.

Sean stopped short at nine hundred miles, nearly halfway, because of a fall that tore his meniscus. At first, it didn't feel like the hike had been long enough. He returned to his family home and had trouble transitioning back, just as Zach did, as all thru-hikers do. Sean's father, Bob, was a lifer in the military, specializing in infantry intelligence. Sean had not shared what happened in the Middle East when he came home between deployments. He said that it was so intense it would scare his parents to hear it. The whole family wanted Sean to get better as quickly as possible. Patricia Resick has explained, however, "PTSD does not go away. It is managed. Although well-meaning family members want their adult [sons and daughters] to get on with their [lives], most don't have a clue as to what it feels like when your brain in hijacked. The trauma was forged into the brain and the soldier is so changed by his experience."

Young veterans regularly observe that the military does an extremely effective job of training them to operate within the military, and an extremely poor job of reversing that training or preparing them to return to civilian life. As Sean said, "They certainly don't prepare you for dealing with death." Healing is an ongoing process, which will continue their entire lives. Wishing returning vets would "just get over it" is unrealistic and impossible. Sean's family worried about him. This time, since he had hiked so many miles, Sean had the language to share his struggle. He was also now older and had more tools and life experiences. He went on to get more helpful therapy.

AS TRAVIS HAD ADVISED, SEAN HAD REPLACED SOME OF HIS BAD MEMORIES with good ones. He had finally cried about his loss. Although Sean stopped short of reaching Mount Katahdin in Maine, he did make long tracks toward his recovery. "That spring on the trail," he said, "I was like a phoenix rising from the ashes." Sean went on to enroll in the National Outdoor Leadership School (NOLS) and participated in a month-long educator course in the Wind River Mountains of Wyoming's Rockies. He secured a position at Glacier National Park, where he spent many days hiking the high country and proudly earned the privilege of wearing a Ranger uniform once again.

CHAPTER 13

DAN STEIN

US ARMY RANGER, 2007–2011

*You'll only meet a few people in your life who are truly
abandoned houses—rundown, worn out, collapsing at the seams.
I'm not asking you to take up a hammer and nails and pin up
their rafters, fix their leaky faucets or put new panes of glass in
their broken windows; I am asking you to simply open their door.
And spend a little time memorizing their floor plan. Get to know
them. And when the time comes, I want you to draw back their
curtains, and once and for all, let the light in.*
—Paulo Coelho

I LIKE TO THINK THAT things happen for a reason, but I had serious doubts in October 2015 when I attended the Appalachian Long-Distance Hikers Gathering at Williams College, in Williamstown, Massachusetts. I lost my purse and after hours of searching, I gave up and began the long drive home. But as I drove it occurred to me that I'd neglected to check at the hotel's front desk. I made the half-hour drive back to the hotel, and, sure enough, someone had turned it in. Of all my friends at the event, I called only one—Travis Johnston—to share the good news.

Travis had just completed hiking the entire Appalachian Trail and was celebrating at the Gathering, catching up with his fellow long-distance-hiker friends. His Ranger friends had watched his transformation through the many photos that Travis posted on Facebook. Spending all that time walking in nature had obviously begun to heal Travis's heart wounds. Soon after he climbed Mount Katahdin, his friends began calling to ask, "Do you think hiking would work for me?" Travis possesses a gift. An extrovert by nature, he is a people person. He talks veteran language and doesn't take any bullshit. His heart is as wide as the ocean, and he is not afraid to shed tears, hug, or tell you flat out, "I love you, man."

This is exactly what struggling veterans need, as well as direction on where and how they might find happiness and peace in their civilian life. After the Gathering, Travis planned to hop a ride to Pennsylvania, stopping to visit a struggling Ranger friend in Reading, which, as it happens, is right down the road from where I grew up. I picked up my purse and Travis and loaned him my car so he could visit Dan Stein.

DAN HAD BECOME A RECLUSE, STAYING IN HIS HOME FOR MONTHS AT A time. He was very depressed and felt as though he was living a nightmare. Dan had served in the military for five years and had three deployments during that time. He was in the same platoon as Travis and Sean Reilly. During a routine training, he had a parachute accident. On a jump, his chute came over the top of another Ranger's and collapsed "like a used grocery bag," Dan said, slamming into the earth from 200 feet up. Dan was busted up inside and suffered internal bleeding, but he was able to recover and remain on active duty. Four months after the accident, however, he wrecked his Triumph Bonneville motorcycle on base. As he described it, he basically stopped his bike with his head. For the next three years, he was in eight different hospitals, psychiatric wards, and rehab centers.

Dan had recently moved to Reading, where he had family and had bought a home. I told Travis to bring him back to our log home, get him out of the city, his house, and his head. It was a stretch for Dan, but he trusted Travis, so he packed his overnight bag and came to our home. We took Dan to nearby Hawk Mountain Sanctuary to see if his aching body could handle the hike. The hike in the beautiful autumn woods did him good. There were people there counting hawks, and although we kept to ourselves, Dan had a short anxiety attack where he had to hold onto our hands and squeeze them until he felt calm and safe again.

Back at our log home, we made a campfire and cooked dinner. Travis and Dan slept soundly and peacefully in our guest cabin. This was the first time Dan had been away from the security of his own home for a long time. That first visit, Dan stayed for two nights and two days. When Dan was leaving, he paused at the door and then abruptly turned around. "October 15," he said. "I will never forget this day for as long as I live. Because on this day, a family reached out to me, who never met me yet welcomed me into their home. That has never happened before, and because of that, I will never forget this day."

I had some upcoming travel and told Dan that I would call him when I returned and take him for a hike. Dan couldn't drive at the time as he had a seizure and was required to wait months before getting behind the wheel again. He told Travis and me that everyone forgets about him—I did not want to be one of those people. A month later, I drove to Reading to fetch Dan. All the blinds in every room of his dark, dismal home were drawn completely shut. Dan opened the blinds, letting in the searing daylight. He showed me the plastic composite mold of his brain, made using an MRI image, that the surgeon had given him. It sported a gaping three-inch-wide hole. A screwed-in titanium plate holds Dan's head together, and a curved six-inch scar with a dent appears on the outside. He calls it his "devil's haircut." A divot in his throat is what remains of his trachea breathing hole. His dark eyes in his handsome face command attention.

DAN AGAIN STAYED AT OUR LOG HOME FOR TWO DAYS AND TWO NIGHTS, but by himself this time. On a longer, more strenuous hike, his back and knees held up with ibuprofen. Dan fetched hay with my husband, which was big step for him, to go off and trust being in Todd's company. We took him to Sam's Club, and as he shopped we shared thoughts with him about a few healthy food choices. He tried to extend himself by talking and laughing with the young women at checkout. Back home, we played 500 Rummy at the kitchen table. Interacting in such close quarters was a huge step, he told us. We teased him and told him to get used to it: he was going to have more experiences, more people to meet, more time in nature ... but small steps.

Over the course of a few months, Dan shared his poetry, using the written word as an outlet for his feelings on war, his accident, and his path to healing. He wrote dozens of deeply moving poems and bravely stood up and recited them at open mics in the area. A yoga instructor offered Dan a free session with a practice designed to help with his traumatic brain injury and his many aches and pains. These new experiences, psychologist Lynne Williams explains, were actually growing specialized projections called dendrites on the neurons of Dan's brain. Every time a human has a new experience, dendrites grow from strands into thicker cables. The more complex the network, the more varied the pathways, the less vulnerable we are to trauma. The older a person becomes, the more connectors they have and the greater their ability to handle trauma. That's one of the reasons why a young soldier's brain has more challenges coping with trauma. Since Dan's brain was badly damaged, all these new experiences helped his brain to heal.

After two short visits with Dan, I observed improvement in him. But setbacks are part of life. A few weeks later, I called to check in. He said he had been sitting and staring at the walls.

"OK," I told him. "I'm coming to pick you up."

"POST-TRAUMATIC STRESS OFTEN RESULTS IN EITHER EMOTIONAL NUMBING or inappropriate anger and irritation," Lynne Williams explains. Problems with emotional regulation are common, and I could see this in Dan. As Dr. Williams put it:

> Either of these extremes will significantly hamper existing relationships or the possibility of future relationships. Sufferers are very often isolated and unconnected emotionally. As Dan denied himself the healthy connection we all need to live well, he also isolated himself from the opportunity to have his very negative perspectives of himself, his future, and the world challenged and changed. Sitting in his darkened, dirty apartment was safe from

experiences and memories that left him feeling out of control, vulnerable, and anxious, but it also constricted his worldview to dullness, boredom, loneliness, and most likely an intensifying of his physical pain since nothing was distracting him from it. Combine all those factors, and life, the world, and the future can all seem pretty discouraging.

Dan asked if I could take him to the trail along the Tulpehocken Creek in Reading, where there is a red covered bridge that he remembered from his childhood. His mother had taken him there when he was about eight years old and he wanted to find it again. I knew the bridge and the trail well. When the long span of the bridge came into view, he exclaimed, "That's it!" We walked through the cool darkness of the bridge, watching light dance on the water through the planks. We took the trail to the exact location where Dan had stood before the war, before the accidents, before the three years in hospitals—back when life was simple. I took his photo. Swiss psychiatrist Carl G. Jung, founder of analytical psychology, talks about a bridge being a healing metaphor in trauma. It symbolizes transitions, crossing over from the unconscious to the conscious. When a bridge drawing shows up in therapy work, Jung wrote, "we can anticipate that inner healing forces are entering and working from the inside." Even though Dan's red bridge was real, it felt like a powerful metaphor.

The snowy trail glinted, reflecting the brilliant cobalt-blue sky. The strikingly white limbs of the sycamores were in sharp contrast. They looked like capillaries with the trunk as the main artery, or a river with its tributaries as if seen from above the planet. I don't think Dan had ever looked at trees like that before. He didn't even know what a sycamore was. I pointed out things in nature, listened to bird songs, saw shadows, encouraging Dan to use all his senses—everything was new, and he couldn't stop taking photos. These kinds of experiences can't happen sitting indoors with the blinds pulled tight, staring at the walls or at a large-screen monitor. As Jung advised in the first volume of his *Letters*: "You must go in quest of yourself, and you will find yourself again only in the simple and forgotten things. Why not go into the forest for a time, literally? Sometimes a tree tells you more than can be read in books." That is the essence of ecotherapy before it had a name.

DAN PLANNED TO SPEND THE WHOLE NEXT DAY WITH ME. I LISTED ALL THE things we would be doing—many potential anxiety-producing experiences. I asked if this was a good idea, and he assured me that it was. He unscrewed the cap from his pill bottle and downed an anxiety pill without water. Next stop was DJ and Loretta Duncan's dairy farm. Dinner would be followed by snowmobiling under a full moon and then a hot tub soak. Shortly after we arrived at their large Robesonia dairy farm, Dan informed me that he had never seen cows being milked. Into the milking parlor DJ led us, but first we had to get through the cow traffic jam. The eighteen-hundred-pound Holstein cows were crammed together, all wanting their turn to get milked. We squeezed through their wide, high bodies, shooing them aside as we waded on the slimy, slippery, manure-covered concrete. I wondered, "Would this cause Dan anxiety?" He sloshed into the parlor, amazed to learn that a suction contraption pulls the milk out of their teats and sends it along a hose to the cooler; then it pops off automatically when the milk has been drained. DJ squirted some foamy, bright-green soap all over Dan when he asked what the colorful pools were beneath the cows' feet. DJ instructed Dan to stick his finger into the udder sucker. It grabbed and squeezed his index finger.

After dinner, bundled up in the moonlight, we climbed aboard the snowmobiles. Dan had to shove an extremely tight motocross helmet over his head—DJ's daughter's pink helmet. Any anxiety? Nope! DJ announced that there were two snowmobiles—a new one and an old one that had no brakes. "I'll go on the snow mobile without the brakes," Dan offered. "You know I like to live on the edge." The moon was brilliant, filling the hillsides around the farm with white light as bright as daylight. Flying over the ice-covered snow and bouncing over bumps, Dan held his arms extended high in the air, as if he was on a roller coaster. No anxiety there. After the action-packed day, Dan offered his services to help on the farm. Extending himself like that was very hopeful. He was engaging in life and nature, meeting new people, placing himself in strange and potentially anxiety-creating situations. He saw the value of it, and it made him happy. It made him feel alive.

THE MORE TIME DAN AND I SPENT TOGETHER, THE MORE HE CAME TO TRUST me. He shared more of his deeper, darker layers. Dan was not physically abused as a child, but he was neglected and ignored. He was not socially adept and was bullied in school. He knew he behaved differently, and he thought differently too. Instead of being celebrated for his uniqueness, he was mocked. He hated school.

When he signed up with the Army, Dan scored unusually high and so he was offered a Ranger contract. He loved being a Ranger and did a very good job. Dan's sergeant major learned that many of the Rangers had taken items from the Afghan homes that they cleared "as a memento." The men rationalized this as "nothing that seemed very valuable in our eyes." Nevertheless, their superior lined up the Rangers and asked the men to go back to their barracks and fetch the mementos. "No one will be punished, nor suffer any repercussions, unless the item was valuable," he promised, so they trusted their superior and brought out the items. It made a large pile. The sergeant major held up items asking which Ranger had lifted it. Dan's religious poster was one of the first to be identified. He wanted to be honest and so he stepped forward and admitted to it.

"Then the sergeant major flipped on us," Dan said "went on a power trip and began yelling that we weren't practicing the Ranger Creed." He stripped Dan of his Ranger badge and demoted him to the Army's 82nd Airborne Division. After that, very few Rangers owned up. "A handful of us were forced to leave the Ranger Battalion that day," Dan said. "It changed everything. It was the start of my new life." The demotion broke his heart and propelled him down a road of self-destruction. He was hugely disappointed and very angry; to cope, he began drinking heavily. He was often under the influence of heavy alcohol, as strong as he could find.

Later that spring, in March 2011 at Fort Bragg, North Carolina, a surprise drill was run for which Dan was not prepared. Paratroopers jump, one after another, in supposedly safe intervals. The paratrooper following Dan was heavier, dropped quicker, and caught up to Dan. His chute created a vacuum and took Dan's air. "It was like falling from a twenty-story building with a paper bag for resistance," he said. Unfortunately, Dan said, he was hung over from the night before and wasn't functioning at 100 percent alertness. He got confused about which cord to pull and for a few seconds went toward the other guy's chute instead of away. He was calm as the ground rushed toward him, rehearsing in his mind how to best plan the impact—feet together, knees slightly bent, fall and roll to one side. By some miracle, Dan suffered no broken bones but did have internal bleeding and years of severe residual pain in his knees, back, and other joints. The chute accident might have occurred anyway, but Dan's actions didn't help.

As a way to cope, Dan grew more angry and disappointed with himself and continued drinking heavily. Three months later, he had his motorcycle wreck. His recollection of the aftermath is harrowing:

> For hours, I laid by the road until a motorist found me in a pool of blood around three a.m., with no pulse. When CPR was finally administered, my heart started back up but at the first hospital they took me to, they said my brain injury was too severe, and they could not treat me. They put me into a medically induced coma. The second hospital's neurosurgeon left me for brain dead. After five to six hours passed from the time of the accident, I woke up from the coma and the nurse went running out to call the surgeon back in. A hole was cut into my head to alleviate the pressure. It is a mystery why I wasn't brain dead.
>
> I was put on a bunch of machines, had feeding tubes attached, but given no painkillers. I was told that with a Traumatic Brain Injury (TBI), I could not have them. I can't even tell you how much pain I was in. It became so bad that I strategically planned how to cut off my legs with a chainsaw just to have it stop. A prosthesis would have been welcomed.

Dan thinks the ventilation tubes created scars in his throat, which then introduced atypical pneumonia and sepsis into his body. The surgeons performed a tracheotomy to help him breathe. He had to relearn how to eat, talk, and walk. What Dan could not manage to figure out, however, was how to live again. He felt abandoned and ignored in the eight different hospitals and rehab facilities he was sentenced to. It took three years for him to recover enough to leave the hospital. Within four months of finally being released, Dan moved to Reading, reconnected with Travis, and then met Todd and me. "I hated myself for my poor choices and was embarrassed to be alive," he said. "I didn't want to talk to anyone. I feared they would hate me if they knew the truth. I tried to kill myself four times, using pills and alcohol."

MONTHS PASSED AFTER DAN'S VISIT TO THE DUNCAN FARM. HIS MENTAL health took a nosedive. He landed in a space that got so painful it scared him. I was scared too, and I felt I needed to get him some outside help. I wrestled with whether it was the right thing to do and how exactly to go about it. In reporting him for care, I feared I'd lose his friendship and trust. In fact, he disappeared from my life for a time. After many months of silence, however, Dan sent a message asking if I had time for a hike. He said he could use some peace.

Tearful with relief, I drove the forty minutes to Reading and brought him to our home. In the car, he caught me up with what had gone down in the previous months of his absence. He had descended to a very dark place but did the most courageous thing a struggling veteran can do—he went into rehab before it was too late. On some different meds now, he seemed to be doing much better, and he had a real solid plan to turn the page.

My nonprofit, River House PA, was holding its monthly hike and potluck campfire. I knew the other veterans and friends would help support Dan. The low evening sunlight in the forest was magical, as shafts of honey-colored rays shot through the canopy, highlighting patches of woods. After a lovely three-mile walk, the group returned to the homestead where Todd had stoked an inviting fire. We brought out covered dishes, roasted hot dogs, toasted marshmallows, and chatted easily, laughing with one another. Dan asked for my guitar, and after tuning it by firelight, serenaded us with sweet melodies, mostly his own compositions. His face transformed in the firelight. Peace and contentment covered it. He stopped playing after a bit and offered some sobering facts of what he had gone through. Most important was having support like this: people to talk to, who listen and care. We assured Dan that we genuinely cared and hoped his health and good spirit continued. When he questioned why his life and happiness mattered to us, we assured him that no matter if we had just met that night or he had been in our lives for a year, Dan mattered.

IN THE MORNING, DAN AND I WENT FOR AN EARLY HIKE ON THE APPALA-chian Trail. His legs and knees, usually stiff and sore, were manageable, at least for the time being. His good mood, sense of peace, and level of happiness had affected his body. Neuroscientist Benedict Kolber at Duquesne

University, Pittsburgh, explains this phenomenon. Kolber claims that exercise actually changes the brain, so it can cope with pain, by manufacturing natural opioids that work the same way as addictive meds to reduce pain. In fact, the brain can make so many of these natural opioids that they can dampen pain and replace it with euphoria. Physical activity alone uses up the stress chemicals released by the activated sympathetic nervous system (what is known as the stress-arousal system), produces the body's natural form of morphine, and stimulates the production of serotonin. This natural form of opiods, produced by exercise, is much better than drinking whiskey or taking opiates. PTSD results in an almost chronic level of arousal of the sympathetic nervous system, but activities in nature help calm the overactive nervous system.

Dan surprised me by mentioning that he was planning a big life move in the upcoming weeks. He had connected with some Ranger friends in Colorado, found a log home in the Rocky Mountains to buy, and hoped to volunteer at the local fire department, learning new skills like forest fire fighting. A veteran's nonprofit there called Regroup for Vets provides free housing for returning vets. He also hoped to volunteer. "It's because of my hikes with you and all this time in nature, that I was able to find my peaceful place," he told me. "I want to live in the mountains. I want to climb higher than I ever have before. I want to climb above tree line and keep going until I am on the top."

CHAPTER 14

JESSE BIER

US MARINE, 1990–2006

Until you heal the wounds of your past, you are going to
bleed. You can bandage with food, with alcohol, with drugs,
with work, with cigarettes, with sex. But eventually, it will
ooze through and stain your life. You must find the strength
to open the wounds. Stick your hand inside, pull out the
core of the pain that is holding you in your past, the
memories, and make peace with them.
—Iyanla Vanzant

IN 2003, STAFF SERGEANT JESSE Bier found himself inside a US Army tank at Camp Commando in the Kuwaiti desert—not to man it, but to clean it out. It had been found upside down in the Euphrates River with dead Marines inside. After the bodies were removed and it was transported back to camp, Jesse donned coveralls and, along with another Marine, began the laborious task of emptying out its contents. Searching for a bullet shell casing, they scraped out mud with their bare hands.

Along the tank commander's hatch, Jesse found colored drawings of the staff sergeant's family, made by his little girl. It was obvious how much she loved her daddy and vice versa. He found photos of loved ones and heartfelt letters. Every letter was carefully read and every photo looked at and categorized by its subject matter. He found a full-size photo album in the driver's hatch. After a while he requested sand buckets like the ones kids use at the beach to empty out the tank's contents. Piles of sand and contents were laid out on a concrete pad in long lines along the Euphrates River. From sunup to sundown for a solid week, Jesse and his buddy worked at cleaning every crack and crevice of the tank. Jesse really got to know the men who had died inside the tank, and it was heartbreaking.

"I can still smell the dank, moldy smell." Jesse can't recall the children's faces in the photographs, and that's a good thing. He has enough personal images for a lifetime of nightmares and anxiety attacks. "I lost other men, one who burned to death. I stood guard over their caskets, watched their mothers mourn at the funerals. I feel all their pain." With three wartime deployments and sixteen years serving in the Marines, trauma for Jesse is a demon that is often present.

JESSE'S TRAUMA DID NOT BEGIN IN AN OVERSEAS WAR BUT IN HIS YOUTH, as a victim of events that occurred before the age of eighteen (known as adverse childhood experiences, or ACEs). These include all types of childhood maltreatment and household dysfunction. Jesse's first memories held fear as he grew up in a very abusive home with his mother and stepfather. At six, he was removed from his home because his mother punched him and broke his nose. Jesse and his sister were placed in a children's home for five years, and he experienced molestation and abuse from the older children in the home. When he was eleven, the state returned him to his parents, and his stepfather began to molest him as well as beat him. At fifteen, he and his stepfather got into a fight, and Jesse was shot in the base of his neck. The bullet hit his scapula, went through his lung, and shattered four ribs as it exited. Soon after, Jesse went into rehab to deal with all the abuse and became homeless at sixteen. During high school, he set his sights on the military as a way of escaping.

According to a 2016 study conducted by Larry Applewhite, PhD, a clinical social worker at Fort Hood, Texas, for *Oxford Military Medicine*, the military often serves as a route for individuals escaping a dysfunctional home. In a review of the behavioral health records of soldiers deployed in the Iraq and Afghanistan wars, 83 percent reported at least one type of ACE and 40 percent reported four or more ACEs. Previous life experiences may contribute to a person's difficulties after combat as well. "Exposure to both ACEs and deployment-related trauma increases the chances of developing postdeployment psychological symptoms," Dr. Applewhite explains. "ACEs have a robust and graded relationship to depression, substance abuse, PTSD, hallucinations, and an increased risk for attempting suicide in adulthood." The military remains a very good place to learn discipline, life skills, and better health, but combat deployments to a war zone have the power to take victims of ACE right back to their original trauma.

While cycling through three combat deployments in the Middle East wars, Jesse's post-traumatic stress grew more severe and extremely complex. In 2004, shortly after Jesse married Caroline, also a Marine, things began to fall apart. He was still in the military as an Ordnance Officer for Second Light Armored Reconnaissance Battalion at Camp Lejeune in North Carolina at the time. As an Ordnance Officer he was responsible for ensuring that weapons systems, vehicles, and equipment were ready and available—and in perfect working order—at all times. He managed the development, testing, fielding, handling, storage, and disposal of munitions (military weapons, ammunition, equipment, and stores), an important job with huge responsibilities. Jesse prided himself on being accurate and responsible, but in his state at the time, he could no longer account for people or weapons. Everything started hitting him emotionally, and he began crying and having outbursts at work. This led to a complete breakdown, landing him in the crisis unit, where he was diagnosed with severe PTSD. They put him on so many meds that all he could do was sit, drooling, with his head in his wife's lap.

He attempted suicide five times between 2005 and 2012, to alleviate the pain. One was an attempted "suicide by cop"—that is, antagonizing the police to try to get them to shoot him. On three different occasions he tried taking pills; the third almost finished him. His kidneys shut down and he went into renal failure. He had to be intubated, where an endotracheal tube is inserted through the mouth and then into the airway. Another time he had gastric lavage administered, which is pumping the stomach using activated charcoal. These attempts were all within a short time span, punctuating a very sad period for Jesse.

Between 2005 and 2012, Jesse was in and out of a dozen psychiatric hospitals and VA hospitals, and enrolled in PTSD therapy and alternative programs. He has tried prolonged exposure therapy, cognitive behavior therapy, and brain blocks. He also experienced month-long transcranial magnetic stimulation (TMS), a noninvasive procedure that uses magnetic fields to stimulate nerve cells in the brain to alleviate symptoms of depression. TMS is typically used as a last resort among other depression treatments. "I spent a half hour in the dark with the lights out," Jesse explained. "I was strapped in a chair and my head was secured in a harness. An electromagnetic coil was attached against my scalp, near my forehead. The powerful magnet charge was turned up very high until my face and all its muscles shook, then they calibrated it and cranked it down until it stopped. The session lasted for half an hour." The magnetic pulse painlessly stimulates the nerve cells in the region of the brain that controls mood and eases symptoms of depression. Jesse feels that TMS was the most successful of all the therapies he experienced, and he remained fairly happy and stable for about two years afterward. These PTSD programs, however, did not help him in the long term.

JESSE ATTEMPTED TO THRU-HIKE THE APPALACHIAN TRAIL FIVE TIMES. HIS first attempts at long-distance hiking were in 2013 and again in 2014, 2015, 2016, and 2018. Jesse initially found out about the AT when he and Carolyn traveled to Clingmans Dome in the Great Smoky Mountains after getting married in Gatlinburg, Tennessee. At 6,644 feet, Clingmans is Tennessee's most elevated point and the highest of the entire 2,192-mile Appalachian Trail. Jesse walked just thirty feet of the trail and said, "So *this* is the AT? I want to hike it!" That was in 2005. He filed away the dream until 2013, when he left the military.

Jesse's life after active duty, before his first thru-hike, was dismal. There was a lot of sitting on the couch, playing video games and watching TV, with blankets on the windows blocking sunlight. He could easily let a month go by and never venture out into the world. His wife would tell him that he needed to get out and go somewhere—anywhere at all—and gave him grocery lists. In 2012, he began to plan to hike the AT. In 2013, Jesse began his first thru-hike from Springer Mountain, Georgia, with his dog, Cooper.

Initially, things did not go very well since he packed way too much gear—sixty-five pounds worth. He carried a foldout shovel, a steel camp chair with canvas cover, and a complete set of AT maps for the entire trail, all the way up to Maine. He also carried food, that he *thought* would be good for backpacking, but it took so long to cook he ended up eating it unheated and raw. At Georgia's Hawk Mountain shelter, three days in, he was so cold and anxious during an ice storm that he could not bring himself to leave. He had a tube tent that provided zero protection from cold and rain, and he had never set it up before his hike began. He barely ate. He was carrying a case of Power Bars, but they were so frozen he could not chew them. A southbound thru-hiker who had two thousand miles on his boots came into the shelter. He looked terrible—emaciated and exhausted; Jesse wondered if this is what was in store for *his* future.

Then at Neel's Gap, thirty miles from the start, Jesse met hiking veterans Steve Clendenning, Stephanie Cutts, Adam Bautz, and Tommy Gathman (all profiled in this book), and his attitude turned around. These veterans knew quite a bit about backpacking, so they went through his gear and trimmed thirteen pounds of stuff that he didn't need, which he mailed home. "My pack felt amazing!" Jesse exclaimed. They told him to ditch the tube tent and get a lightweight backpacking tent. "I loved my new tent. It was my safe spot. I enjoyed the quiet, peering out and looking around. There is something about traveling on the trail, setting up your tent at day's end—there is a comfort about it." The goal was to start to feel comfortable enough on the trail, in the woods, carrying a backpack, covering the miles, that the peace could begin to permeate his being. Jesse said:

> I love the feeling of being physically exhausted—after you get your trail legs and your body feels so athletic and everything is working like a machine. I love the endorphins that surge through your body. I like to hike fast, and go as far as I can in a day. There is something so satisfying about all that physical exertion. I sleep so well on the trail, rarely having a nightmare. I was mentally exhausted too, for there's a lot to think about. I watched the weather, I calculated miles and where I was planning to stop for the night, as well as my next resupply point. I thought about my calories, whether I was getting enough protein, etc. My mind was very busy.

THIS PERIOD ON THE AT WAS THE FIRST TIME SINCE SUFFERING WITH PTSD that Jesse felt he could take care of himself. Until this point, his wife had been his caregiver. She got him up every day, gave him a list of things to do to get him moving. But on the trail, Jesse got himself up and looked forward to hiking. "The AT is about adventure," he said. "I even loved the planning of it beforehand, as well as the execution of the journey. I love being in wilderness. There is one particularly beautiful place on the trail when you're about to go into the Smoky Mountains. It's a pine forest and the sunlight beams coming through the trees is so soft. It's dark and cool in there and it smells so good. I can remember that day, and how good I felt. This is what the trail means to me, what it does for me."

Although he did not know it, Jesse was benefiting from the medicinal aerosols that the evergreens were releasing into the air that he was breathing. In the documentary film *The Call of the Forest: The Forgotten Wisdom of Trees*, visionary scientist and author Diana Beresford-Kroeger explains that these airborne organic compounds called phytoncides, or wood essential oils, have antibacterial and antifungal properties and prompt the body to boost the immune system by stimulating the production of NK (natural killer) cells, which attack infection and guard against disease. They also make us feel good.

That first year, Jesse made it as far as Front Royal, Virginia, before getting off the trail, having successfully covered nearly a thousand miles. He has returned to the trail four more times, bringing other wounded warriors along with him. His groups always stopped short of reaching their goal of Mount Katahdin in Maine, because the other veterans slowed Jesse down, which was a strain on him. Long-distance hiking is not for everyone, and there needs to be a certain level of passion in your heart for the sport, or you won't be able to muscle (both physically and mentally) through the hard parts. One or two veterans were still struggling with substance abuse, which Jesse didn't know about at the time.

Jesse realized that he could not be responsible for getting others up the trail—it's too much work. "I just wanted someone else, another wounded warrior to feel/experience the freedom and joy that I felt in the woods, hiking the trail." But Warren Doyle, who completed the entire AT seventeen times and created the Appalachian Long-Distance Hikers Association and the Appalachian Trail Institute, has some advice about the sport: "Don't fight the trail. You have to flow with it. You can't make a mountain any less steep or an afternoon any cooler or the day any longer, so don't waste your energy complaining. Time and distance and terrain and the trail itself cannot be changed. You have to change yourself. You have to adapt your heart, mind and soul to the trail. For every five days on the trail, you can expect one day to be uncomfortably wet, one day to be uncomfortably dry, one day to be uncomfortably hot, one day to be uncomfortably cold, and one day to be comfortable."

JESSE'S SERVICE DOG, COOPER, A LARGE YELLOW LAB FROM K9S FOR Warriors, shared every mile of trail for every one of his thru-hikes. The organization provides canines to warriors who suffer from PTSD as a result of their military service after 9/11. They aim to empower veterans to return to civilian life with dignity and independence. Cooper is an Assistance Dogs International (ADI) certified service dog. ADI is a worldwide coalition of nonprofit programs that train and place assistance dogs. ADI establishes and promotes standards of excellence in the areas of assistance in dog acquisition, training, and partnership. When Jesse met Cooper, the dog was less than a year old and had been in training for much of that time. Jesse enrolled in a three-week program in a live-in facility in Florida, and the pair began their day at 8:00 a.m. when they would go into the public and learn to work together in the world.

"He is a goofball," said Jesse, "a very warm, smart dog with a definite sense of humor." At six feet two inches and close to two hundred pounds, Jesse had wanted a large dog. "I would look ridiculous with a little dog. Plus, if I needed him to help me get up, he needed to be a big dog." At first, Jesse found it challenging to hike with Cooper. The dog was trained to hike beside him, which was difficult while Jesse used hiking poles. Most long-distance hikers use poles because they significantly reduce stress on your knees and back, and they help with balance and prevent falls. With three or four points of contact, negotiating tricky terrain also becomes easier. Where Jesse would naturally place his pole, however, is right where Cooper's body would be. He had to aim and place the pole around his dog's head with every step. So he had to teach Cooper to walk a pace or two behind him and to sling the twelve-foot hands-free lead over his shoulder. It didn't take long before the pair figured it out.

Cooper carries his own dog food on the trail in a great pack, called the "Long Howl," exclusively made and donated by the company Granite Gear. There are two removable saddlebags that attach to Cooper's working vest. On the trail Jesse feeds Cooper dried dog food two times a day, supplemented with jerky and extra-virgin olive oil. The team carried about five days' worth of food before resupplying.

MOST LONG-DISTANCE HIKERS ARE GOOD PEOPLE, BUT EVERY NOW AND then Jesse met someone on the trail who seemed a little shady. Cooper would sense this immediately and place himself between that person and Jesse. "This rarely happened," Jesse admitted. "Most folks who hike are great people. In fact, hiking has restored my faith in humanity and helped me with trust issues," a struggle many veterans share. If Jesse says the command, "Brace!" Cooper comes over to Jesse and stands there so he can push up on his withers between his shoulders and help Jesse get up. On the trail, when they had to drop far into the valley off a ridge to obtain water from a spring, Jesse would give the command "Up Cooper!" and he'd help pull him up the mountain. "He weighs ninety-five pounds!" Jesse said. One time, Cooper performed over and above the call of duty of a service trail dog. Down in the Southern Appalachians, the black bear population can be thick. One particular night, Jesse, having hung his food bag in a tree, high in the air, about twenty-five yards away, was awakened by a growling bear rummaging around outside his tent. Jesse leashed Cooper to his leg and placed him outside his tent so Cooper could keep the bear at bay. All night long the growling and barking and harassing went on as Jesse drifted in and out of sleep, confident in his dog's ability to keep him and the food safe. In the morning, the tree the food was hanging in had claw marks and tufts of fur on its bark, but the food sack remained unscathed and the food inside intact. Cooper had done a great job as a guard dog!

After all the miles, is another thru-hike in Jesse's near future? "I'm thinking about it," he said. "I am *really* thinking about it. I'd start in Pennsylvania, the farthest I reached in my five thru-hiking attempts, and go from there. I could use another long hike. I still have trauma. I have regret and guilt. I can't change the past but I wish I could. Maybe I could have done something differently, or do something that I didn't do, or perhaps have been a better Marine. I haven't forgiven myself yet for some of the things that happened or didn't happen over there." With Jesse's sixteen years of military service and his long line of seventeen military medals, including Navy and Army Commendation Medals, no one would doubt that he wasn't a fine Marine and always tried to do his best. Plus, he is one of the kindest, warmest, most gentle men you'd ever want to meet. His trauma has not eroded his heart, and he always gets up when he is down.

> I try not to think about my military trauma. It's intrusive and annoying to have it resurface and have to look at it again and again. The coping mechanisms I've been taught to use when these bad feelings arise works for a while, and then they stop. The trail is where I find the most peace and relief. I don't feel like a loser. I certainly have been trying, in life, and on the trail. On a scale of one to one hundred in personal happiness, I feel I am about seventy percent. That's not bad for a veteran who is rated at one hundred percent disabled! I think the next time I try a thru-hike, I might be able to pull it off and get all the way to [Mount] Katahdin.

JESSE AND COOPER HAVE LOGGED ABOUT FOUR THOUSAND TRAIL MILES. That's a lot of time spent on the trail—a lot of healing going on.

CHAPTER 15

GABE VASQUEZ

US MARINE CORPS, 2006–2014

GABE VASQUEZ'S TRAUMA DID NOT start on the plane coming back from his last Afghanistan deployment, but his seatmate on that flight sure ramped it up. Gabe wore his Marine uniform, which was a dead giveaway that he was returning from the war. His seatmate, who believed she was psychic, said she knew what had happened during Gabe's deployment. She said she had a direct line to the Almighty. This disturbed passenger took it upon herself to condemn the Marine, who had just finished up his third tour. It had been a hugely traumatizing deployment: trucks blowing up, buddies dying, resulting in physical and moral injury. The kind of stuff "a shitload of Purple Hearts are given out for," Gabe said. The woman verbally ripped him apart, spewing vicious accusations with a raised, nasty voice, telling him flat out that God would never forgive him, even if Gabe begged for forgiveness, for what he had done in Afghanistan, and that Gabe and the rest of the military fighting the war would all burn in hell.

The flight attendant quickly moved Gabe into first class, apologizing profusely for the woman's abominable behavior. The outburst of that unhinged seatmate left long-lasting psychological trauma on Gabe. "She pretty much had me convinced she was right," he said. It has taken him years and many thousands of miles to come back from the dark place into which he descended. But climb he has.

ALTHOUGH GABE HAD BEEN IN THE MARINES FOR A TOTAL OF EIGHT YEARS and deployed to Iraq, he said "shit was different" after his time in Afghanistan. He was trained to be a tanker in Iraq, but three months before deployment to Afghanistan, his job changed to route clearance, or, as he explained it, "the stupidest job there was. We either found the IEDs first, drove over them, or stepped on them." As a sergeant, Gabe had to send his guys out on the roads on foot with metal detectors to find bombs. A few did not return. That just about destroyed him. He felt responsible for them. "Every day you ask yourself, 'Is it gonna happen today? Is today the day that I die? We played the lottery every single day. Every bush we walked by could be the one that gets us." He and many of his Marines asked themselves, "What the fuck are we doing here?"

When he returned home, Gabe struggled with sleep, avoiding it for as long as he could, functioning on only a few hours a night. Nearly every evening his dead comrades returned to him in his nightmares. He remembered everything about the worst explosion he experienced in detail. He relived what happened over and over again: the Humvee moving ahead real slow, then leaving it behind, looking for a trip wire, not finding it, and then the IED blowing up the truck and his men—his boys, since some were only eighteen years old. In his tortured mind, Gabe tried to decide if it was possible to have done it any differently. He also dreamed about other trucks that were blown up, which he watched from his own truck window.

The herniated disc he received when the explosion blew him airborne causes tremendous pain. Combined with the pain in his heart, it drove him to try to kill himself slowly with alcohol and pills. The VA had him on a dozen different meds. "I became an alcoholic and a pill junkie. I did anything that would prevent me from dealing with my pain." Many a morning after a night of consuming large amounts of pills and alcohol he was surprised to find that he was still alive. Gabe was stuck in his trauma because he was avoiding processing his experiences and the emotions involved.

It got really bad while Gabe was working as a recruiter. "I was great at the job, but I started drinking during work hours, and as soon as my shift was done, I busted out the pills, crushed them on my desk, and snorted them. The dreams were driving me crazy. I learned that when you black out, you don't dream. I also learned that when I took more meds and mixed them all, I was so high that I forgot about Afghanistan for a little while." Gabe always kept his guns loaded, even when he was drunk and high. "Once, I was so mad and fucked up, I went outside my apartment and began shooting my shotgun. Then I went inside and inserted my pistol into my mouth and actually pulled the trigger. I was done. I gave up," he said. Unbeknownst to him, an "angel" friend, the other recruiter, had unloaded it. He and his wife regularly checked on Gabe to check that he was still breathing when he passed out, and made sure he got up to go to work every day.

"I realized how dumb I was acting and I got real scared. I hit bottom," Gabe said. "I went cold turkey and flushed all my meds down the toilet. That was one of the worst experiences of my life, going through withdrawal. I almost killed myself doing that." Since then, Gabe has not allowed a single pill to touch his lips, not even a Tylenol. Forced in 2014 to honorably retire early from the military, after nineteen years of service, Gabe knew something was very wrong with him. He had tried traditional therapy administered by the VA. He knew pills were not the answer. Instead, Gabe sought a different type of therapy: he is crossing America, again and again and again, until he feels better, and he's not stopping anytime soon.

GABE'S FIRST CROSSING WAS A KAYAK TRIP DOWN THE MISSISSIPPI RIVER in 2014. A friend of Gabe's, Nic Doucette, told him that he was going to paddle the entire river, source to gulf, and raise money and awareness for wounded veterans. "I called up Nic and told him I was gonna do it with him." Gabe got out of the Marines on June 3, 2014, and on June 4 he was in Minnesota buying gear and getting ready to launch. Neither Gabe nor Nic knew anything about paddling. They took crap they did not need, such as a full-sized cot. Gabe's gear weighed a good one hundred pounds, and Nic carried two hundred pounds. Gabe flipped his kayak going over an unsuspected dam one day and lost gear. "But I had so much shit, and so many doubles of things," he laughed, "that it didn't matter."

They set out to run a spillway, but Gabe's boat got stuck on the dam. He was thrown out of his boat and went over the dam. The swirling water spun him around and slammed him into the concrete barrier on the river bottom. Once he surfaced and swam to shore, he had to go back out to retrieve his boat. All this was taken in stride, as he related these stories. Every challenge in Gabe's present life was compared to his horrific wartime experiences and his unhealthy way of coping by using drugs and alcohol. Everything else paled in comparison and felt manageable.

The Mississippi River starts out intimate and forgiving. It is born in a national wildlife refuge and abounds with islands, waterfowl, and wildlife. At first Gabe did not realize that he didn't have to keep a death grip on the paddle as he had been doing, making his hands freeze up in a grip even while he slept. After a few hundred miles, he learned to relax his grip and enjoy himself. After two weeks, Gabe felt comfortable on the water. "Paddling is the easiest of all the sports," he said. "Sometimes the river's current will just take you, so you can float and all you have to do is a little ruddering. It's also very peaceful."

The pair averaged about thirty miles a day initially, and their biggest day was eighty-six miles. Gabe raised nearly $18,000 on the seventy-one-day paddle. He said, "I had no idea how much that paddle would change my life. I decided to commit to covering over twenty-seven thousand miles of hiking, kayaking, and cycling to raise money and awareness for wounded vets." He named his mission "Crossing America for Injured Veterans." While he builds awareness of the struggles of combat veterans and their high rate of suicide, he raises money to help them out, donating it to the nonprofit Semper Fi, which helped out a few of his Marine buddies who had lost limbs in the wars. Gabe formally partnered with Semper Fi, and the organization began to manage all the donations that came in. He never handles money himself and uses his own funds from a part-time job operating a tow-motor operation in Austin, Texas, to fuel his crossings. Gabe had gained a sense of meaning and purpose, born out of his suffering and the suffering he witnessed.

AFTER PADDLING THE LENGTH OF THE MISSISSIPPI RIVER, GABE SET HIS sights on hiking the 2,600-mile Pacific Crest Trail. "I didn't even know there were trails that long," he recalled. "At first, I thought it was dumb to walk that far. But I figured it would be so unusual that I could probably get people to donate money to my cause." As with kayaking, Gabe knew nothing about backpacking. He went into a backpacking store and asked the clerk, "This is what I want to do, so what do I need?" Fortunately, the clerk had hiked the PCT himself three years before and offered some good advice. The Pacific Crest Trail kicked Gabe's ass. By today's ultralight standards, his pack was heavy in pounds, in the low forties. Gabe took longer than most thru-hikers to cover the miles—more than six months—but he needed to take forty zero days off to deal with the pain that radiated from his herniated disc and the swelling it caused. Plus, he figured he wrecked other parts of his body, because he changed his walking biomechanics as he compensated for the pain. But he finished the trail and collected $4,000 to $5,000 in donations.

Gabe was excited about his next crossing: cycling across the northern tier of America. When it came time to plan his bike ride in 2017, once again, Gabe did barely any planning and just winged it. When he complained to the owner of a bike shop that a regular bike hurt his back after only a short amount of time, he was introduced to a recumbent bike, which caused him no pain when he rode. His biggest day on his first crossing was 116 miles. He only had one semi-scary encounter on all his crossings, and it was on his bike in Illinois "where I was surrounded by corn and there aren't a lot of brown people like me." (Gabe is Mexican American.) A pick-up truck deliberately got too close to his bike, even though Gabe rode far over on the rumble strip. The driver stopped abruptly after slammed on his brakes and sat in his vehicle staring at Gabe through his rearview mirror. Gabe stopped his bike and stared back. He unzipped his handlebar bag where he carried a pistol, and the driver took off.

In 2017, Gabe hiked across the state of Mississippi to raise money for the nonprofit Warrior Bonfire. With Marine veterans from Desert Storm, the group hiked 155 miles in five days and raised $8,000. This took Gabe's total raised for veterans to $28,000.

As he had for other long trails, Gabe did not plan his food resupply on the Appalachian Trail in 2018. Instead, he headed to a discount grocery in Pennsylvania and found a good deal. He purchased two cardboard banana boxes full of bars—granola bars, multigrain bars, and powerbars. He examined the packaging and nothing was outdated. He rationed six bars for each day, which came out to one cent per bar. The supply contained enough bars to get him all the way to Maine. The two boxes totaled only twenty dollars!

ON THE APPALACHIAN TRAIL, GABE STILL SUFFERED FROM FREQUENT nightmares. He slept in his tent most of the time and avoided the community shelters. The AT is the most crowded of all the nation's trails. An average of four thousand hikers attempt to cover the more than two thousand miles in one shot every calendar year. "That's way too many people for a veteran who is challenged with post-traumatic stress," Gabe said. If he couldn't tent it and had to share a shelter, he told his fellow thru-hikers: "If I talk in my sleep, don't wake me." He frequently woke himself up from yelling. These nightmares occurred less frequently on the AT—about two to three times a week, as opposed to nearly every night before he began his Cross America expeditions.

When Gabe came through Pennsylvania on the Appalachian Trail, Todd and I hosted him at our log home. I picked him up in nearby Port Clinton to administer some "trail magic" and hear his story. At the town pavilion, his friend was braiding his long, sleek black hair into two pigtails. It was hard to imagine this sweet-faced Marine doing dark deeds and seeing such sad sights that he had near nonstop nightmares. At the picnic table that night, by the glow of a campfire, over cups of tea, Gabe spoke about his struggle. "If I told you what I've done, you wouldn't like me," he said. "I didn't talk with my family or friends about what happened over there. They wouldn't understand and they would worry about me if they knew how badly I felt. People are antimilitary, antiwar, antiviolence. They don't want to hear what we have to say." On the trail, Gabe grappled with disturbing memories and whether he'd be able to forgive himself. "I figure I'll think about it until I get over it," he mused.

The AT experience took him by surprise. It has the most challenging climbs of any trail in the country, particularly in New Hampshire's White Mountains, but there were way too many people on the trail for his comfort. He was looking forward to the 3,100-mile Continental Divide Trail, up next.

THE CONTINENTAL DIVIDE TRAIL WAS GABE'S FIRST CROSSING OF AMERICA where he didn't just wing it. The Rockies experienced a record snow-fall in 2019, so Gabe wanted to do a little planning. If he couldn't hike through the 12,000-foot high San Juan Mountains in southern Colorado, he wanted a Plan B. After covering thirteen thousand miles in over four years, Gabe had an epiphany: "I thought about my time in Afghanistan and finally concluded that I could not possibly have done anything differently," he said. "I could not have prevented my buddies' injuries and deaths. Out on the trail, I tried to get it out of me," as if his pain was a swollen abscess under his skin. His sore was open and draining now; there was no more infection.

"For years I forced myself to think about everything that happened over there," he realized, "but I couldn't change a thing. I want to be done with that shit. I can't let it bother me anymore. I needed a new way of thinking, a way to accept my past."

Gabe still doesn't know what to believe—whether what they did in the Middle East did any good or not. That has been the source of angst for many veterans. They struggle with guilt and confusion over a sense of purpose, still trying to avoid accepting that many awful things are beyond their control. As Gabe hiked the Continental Divide Trail, he gained insight into his past behavior. "I have been an asshole to some people in my past," he acknowledged. "I just didn't care. I was mad. I was frustrated with my past and my present life. I was a shitty friend. But I have a better understanding now. I am not as mad. I used to think that no one but fellow vets could understand me or how I feel, but I have changed this belief. I have such wonderful friends from the trail and they are really there for me." Like other veterans profiled in this book, Gabe found a new tribe on the trail, and his relationship with them was similar to the one with his battle buddies.

"It's been a rough couple of years," he admitted. "I want the future to be different." In a Facebook post while hiking the CDT, Gabe wrote: "As I walk these mountains, I start thinking about how much I wish I knew my friends were hurting. I know these trails and being out in nature would have helped them the way it has helped me. My hope is that sharing with you, more people might hear my story and be able to find the help that they need, and ultimately, I might be able to save someone's life." It seemed that suicide was everywhere.

While hiking the Appalachian Trail, Gabe's best Marine buddy who was in Afghanistan with him died by suicide. "Drew wasn't my first close friend who's done that," he said. "But that one hit home because we were really close. He was like my little brother. I spoke with him just three days before he killed himself and I told him he would be okay. I told him to join me on the CDT and everything will be okay. . . . I don't know if it's my fault. I could have done a lot more to help him."

Another Marine buddy drove twelve hours from Ohio to Maine to pick up Gabe on the AT to take him to the funeral. Other Marines who were on the trail with Gabe at the time got off with him to accompany their hurting brother, even though the hikers did not personally know the fallen Marine. While Gabe was on the Pacific Crest Trail, two Marines he knew killed themselves within two weeks. Right before he began the Continental Divide Trail hike, another friend he had fought alongside in Afghanistan killed himself. This particular Marine had started a suicide awareness Facebook page and had made Gabe the administrator, so his death took everyone by surprise. On the CDT, Gabe dedicated each of the five states' trail traverses to five of his Marine buddies who died by suicide. This included two young men whom he talked into signing up when Gabe worked at the recruiting center in his final years in the military. "I brought them into this lifestyle," he said.

THE DOWNTIME SPENT BETWEEN THE CROSSINGS HAVE ALWAYS BEEN A struggle for Gabe. He returns to his home in Austin and gets his old job back as a tow-motor driver. He then saves up enough money to cross America yet another time. Gabe has completed all three National Scenic long-distance hiking trails—the Appalachian Trail, Pacific Crest Trail, and Continental Divide Trail—earning him the prestigious Triple Crown of hiking. What remains of his original plan of cycling the twelve-thousand-mile perimeter of America is a Southern tier bike traverse, an East Coast bike trip, and a paddle down the Missouri and Ohio Rivers, both of which dump into the Mississippi, which he will follow two more times to the Gulf.

> Achieving the Triple Crown meant a lot to me. I cried, because I thought of the veterans and my friends I've lost to suicide. After every trip, I return happier and more humble. I find more peace. I haven't gotten to the point where I've said "I'm done with this shit." I still love it out there. I'm not fast at any of these sports, but I keep going. My attitude with everything is, I'll figure it out. I'll just adapt to everything. The VA tells me not to do these trips, because it is too strenuous for my body. But I don't want to stand still. I'll

become like those old veteran dudes that I see in the VA hospital. Out here is my medication and I don't do these trips for myself.

WITH THOUSANDS OF MILES UNDER HIS BELT, GABE'S FAVORITE WAY TO move across America is hiking. He loves walking best even though it is harder on his body than cycling or paddling. "I feel like I'm closer to nature when I walk." It makes sense that hiking produces the most beneficial results for Gabe, because the movement actually diminishes the whole act of ruminating and obsessing over negative thoughts. A study in the *Proceedings of the National Academy of Sciences* in 2012 showed that hiking in nature reduces neural activity in the subgenual prefrontal cortex, the area of the brain related to mental illness. Psychologists Ruth Ann Atchley and David L. Strayer measured brain activity post-hiking using MRI technology and found that walking in nature reduces mental fatigue, soothes the mind, and boosts creative thinking. Unfortunately the benefits of this research have yet to reach many suffering veterans. Much of the research has been met by the mainstream medical community with resistance. Edward Group, founder of the Global Health Center, says, "There's a great deal of dissent among medical professional when it comes to natural health, and many refuse to entertain the idea that healing involves more than pharmaceutical chemicals."

Like other hiking veterans, Gabe never dreamed he'd find another band of brothers and sisters who would come to feel like his family, like his military buddies. There are not many Mexican Americans on the trails, he's discovered. He believes he is the first to kayak the Mississippi, and one of the tiny handful who completed the Triple Crown. He laments there are not more people of color on the trails. To all his brothers and sisters who are out there hurting, he offers this alternative: "I just want to remind you that you are not alone. I love you all and it hurts me knowing a lot of you are out there fighting these demons alone. I've been there before and given up. There is an alternative. Your life doesn't have to end. There is so much more, and you can definitely find peace. With the help of my brothers and the outdoors, I bounced back and I know you can too."

After the Continental Divide Trail hike, Gabe began to find peace. With his time on the Appalachian Trail, he said he felt 50 percent healed. After all the miles, he admitted that his happiness meter was up to 65 percent, maybe even 70 percent. "I know I'll never reach 100 percent. Part of me died over there and I will never get it back. But I think I can learn to be happy again." Gabe is shooting for 80 percent. A few more crossings should just about do it.

CHAPTER 16

THE BAMBA BOYS

CHRIS KAAG (US MARINE CORPS, 2002–2005)

ERIC KAAG (US MARINE CORPS, 1997–2001)

JOHN PACHARIS (US MARINE CORPS, 1992–1996)

FELIX (PONCHO) PENA (US ARMY, 1968–1971)

CHRIS KAAG WANTED TO BE a Marine his whole life. His grandfather, father, and uncle were all Marines, and Chris loved the sense of pride being a part of the military branch evoked. Boot camp was the hardest experience that he ever endured. His drill instructor had put him out front in a four-and-a-half-mile run, and Chris was doing steady cadence with the rest of the platoon behind him. Then the instructor yelled, "Cadence is done! Pick it up!" Chris had slowed down because his shin splints were incredibly painful, but he heard, "Don't quit on me, Kaag!" Chris did not know that he could be a leader until that moment. He had no way of knowing what fate had in store for him.

When Chris was a twenty-one-year-old Marine and overseas in the Bosnia conflict, he began to experience weird sensations in his legs when running—they were dragging and his hip flexors felt very weak. His physical fitness test results came back five minutes slower than the previous year, and the military doctor diagnosed "foot drop," a weakness or paralysis of the foot muscles which prevents lifting of the front part of the foot. The doctors also thought he might have a tumor on his spine. Chris was medevaced out to Germany and spent nine weeks at Walter Reed National Military Medical Center in Bethesda, Maryland, where the neurology department took spinal taps, looked at possible B12 deficiency, and then just threw up their hands. They had no idea what was going on. The Physical Evaluation Board said that Chris could be in a wheelchair in five years. "It was a punch in my face for a cocky twenty-one-year-old US Marine," Chris recalled.

Walter Reed sent him to the nearby Kennedy Krieger Institute in Maryland, a children's hospital that specializes in spinal cord issues among other debilitating diseases. They found a spot on Chris's neck that indicated a demyelinating disease called adrenomyeloneuropathy (AMN). The marker of this disease is the myelin cover on the nerve is destroyed, which eventually takes away the ability to walk. The condition is the result of a recessive X-link gene passed on from the mother. Relieved to know what was wrong, Chris ramped up daily gym workouts with the strong hope of combating the disease. "Hope is better than fear," he said.

In Krieger, Chris saw many children with breathing tubes, confined to beds, and it moved him to tears that they would never have the childhood he had enjoyed. He decided to never feel sorry for himself. "There are so many others far worse-off than me," he said. In a recovery facility, in a controlled environment, everything is handicapped accessible, he explained, and you are waited on hand and foot. But life outside will be very different moving forward, and you need to find new hobbies or do old hobbies in a different way. After receiving his diagnosis, Chris made a decision: "I could either give up and let my condition control my life, or I could dig in deep and push on. I chose the latter. I decided to view my disability as a stepping-stone and not as a crutch."

Chris attended college at Penn State Berks in Reading where he had to walk with two canes, so he would not trip and fall. He graduated with a degree in business management marketing and held a fundraiser for nerve damage research. From never organizing a thing in his life, Chris attracted 386 participants in a triathlon, raising $16,000—all of which he gave to research. From the back of his pickup truck, Chris created a mobile gym, which he operated entirely outdoors. In 2006 he opened Corps Fitness in Reading, Pennsylvania, a 4,300-square-foot facility. "I always wanted to be a drill instructor," he said, "and now I get to wear civilians out! I don't tolerate excuses. You don't tell a guy in a chair that you can't do something."

Chris learned how expensive it is to be disabled. In response, he launched his foundation, IM ABLE, in 2007. The foundation raises funds to secure recreational equipment to give adaptive individuals the opportunity to discover new possibilities. Chris has given out hundreds of items of adaptive sports gear, including large, expensive pieces like adaptive skis, mountain bikes, road bikes, recumbent bikes, and basketball wheelchairs. A heavy, fifty-pound adaptive mountain bike can cost $10,000. The foundation's slogan is "No excuses. Just move." IM ABLE changes attitudes about the potential of disabled individuals by redefining what is possible.

In 2018, Chris began a new program within the foundation called IM FIT. Corps Fitness offers workshops and classes for anyone, but specifically it provides fitness classes for folks with multiple sclerosis (MS), spina bifida, autism, and Down syndrome. Both children and young adults with every type of physical, mental, and emotional disability are welcomed. The classes are free and are held two times a week. There are between twenty and thirty children who take advantage of the program. Many of the gym's members come in to lend a hand with the kids. After every session there is a dance party.

IT IS STRANGE, BUT WHEN YOU FIRST SEE CHRIS ROLL HIMSELF UP IN HIS wheelchair, which he has been in since he was twenty-five, you don't focus on the chair, but on the dynamic, vibrant, confident, strong individual. "You might see some challenges and differences when you see me," he says, "but everyone has challenges and it depends on the perspective through which you view them. Just because you perceive something different between us, it does not mean that I am prevented from living a fulfilled, inspiring life." Chris aims to "lead from the front," in true Marine fashion, just like when he led his platoon in a cadence run at the young age of seventeen. "I would be a pretty arrogant person if I felt sorry for myself. There are so many that are far worse off than me. I don't have time to worry about myself. So many people limit themselves. They place themselves in a box, when they could really accomplish so much more. I have a big purpose in life. I cannot worry about my own shit."

Chris wants to motivate others, disabled and able-bodied, to redefine the way they view their own personal challenges. "Sixty-one million Americans, one out of four, live with a disability. One million require the assistance of a chair. We all have obstacles, but it is how we respond that makes us who we are. I would not be the person I am today, I would not have the life perspective I have today, had these things not happened to me. Some of my best relationships with people have resulted from these challenges. It might sound strange, but I feel as if I have been saved. I am still a Marine and I am still serving but in a different way."

His new program at the gym, Operation Lead from the Front, is designed to heal military veterans from their personal war trauma. Chris gives them the same opportunity that he had, helping others in worse shape than himself. For example, he partners a wounded warrior with a disabled child and teaches them to motivate each other, push themselves, and lead. An instant connection is made. "The veterans need a next mission and I give it to them."

ERIC KAAG, CHRIS'S YOUNGER BROTHER, SERVED AS A MARINE COMBAT engineer and worked construction on bridges and demolition. Being two years younger than Chris, Eric watched his brother's AMN disease surface and progress. He braced himself for what might well be his fate. He saw signs of the disease in his own body when he was almost thirty years old. A dozen years later, however, the disease did not progress the way it had in his brother. Eric can still get around for short distances away from his vehicle, but he always keeps his wheelchair in the back. Like Chris, he drives a vehicle with hand controls.

"There is a certain amount of stress involved with losing your mobility," Eric says, "stress on your body, stress on your family because they too are impacted by this degeneration, and stress on your psyche as you lose the free life you've been used to." He also has residual stress resulting from his four years of work in law enforcement as a police officer. He was immersed in some real sadness, like deaths and accidents—carrying a two-month-old baby that had died in his arms out of a home, and in another incident, carrying a two-year-old boy who had died. Even though neither Eric nor Chris experienced trauma from their military careers, their lives have certainly been impacted. "It is an enduring disappointment that I cannot do the things I used to do. I see changes every year, where I am not able to do what I could do the year before. I don't hold a pity party, however. I find ways to readjust and move on."

Chris introduced his brother to road handcycles shortly after Eric lost his mobility. Eric got his own bike and stuck to the smooth, fairly level pathways for riding. Then he joined the Berks Area Mountain Bike Association (BAMBA), the local mountain biking club in Reading, Pennsylvania, which got him cycling in the mountains. Eric kneels to cycle. To get on or into his bike, he must grab his knee and lift it over the seat and into position. Eric's body is distributed over his bike seat and the knee cups that cradle his knees. He can shift around a bit as he leans more on his knees to climb a hill, and he can sit back on his butt and get pressure off his knees when he rides downhill. Two hours is about his limit in the saddle before he gets uncomfortable, and he can't easily take a break during a ride. He might stop and stretch out his leg, but he doesn't bring along his cane, which he needs to help him get off the bike.

To move the bike forward takes beastly upper body strength. Eric's strong arms bulge out of their short sleeves when he bends over to crank his cycle. He said that on a thirty-mile road ride, there is a lot of cranking going on to push your body and your bike forward in space. Eric rode a mountain bike in his youth, like his brother, and grew up romping around the woods with his family. Their father was really into hiking and always had a younger sibling in a pack on the family's hikes into the woods. They climbed the Pinnacle on Pennsylvania's Appalachian Trail on a regular basis. Eric camped with his buddies as a teen and always loved his time in the natural world. But when his degenerative disease began to dominate his life, he knew walking with canes on an uneven hiking trail was not safe. He relinquished his time spent in the forest and stayed away for eight years.

JOHN PACHARIS, VETERAN AND FORMER POLICE OFFICER, CHANGED ERIC'S world. A physically challenged cyclist himself, Pacharis shared his handcycle mountain bike that has an electric assist. The bike's drivetrain has a push button that drops the gears into a super-low gear to climb over obstacles. The electrical assist allows even quadriplegics to ride. On an adaptive bike that does not have this feature, a cyclist is really limited as to where he can ride. No steep climbing or riding on really rough terrain is possible because it is so difficult using a hand-cranked wheel. Where this bike could take Eric changed his life. Sometimes, you do not know what you are missing until it reenters your life and reminds you how starved and deprived you have been without it.

That's what Eric experienced when he took to the mountain-biking trails around Reading on an adaptive bike powered with an electronic assist. "Immediately, a deep sense of peace and quiet filled me," Eric said. "I remembered from years back how being in the forest made me feel and I missed it badly. It was almost like I got back a little of who I was before I lost use of my legs, when I could roam and hike at my leisure. It is almost like I can walk again. On my bike, all I feel is that I am moving and I do not even think about not being able to move my legs." Since Eric got his adaptive mountain bike, he hits the trails all the time. He is now able to take his kids, who are six and ten, out mountain biking. His wife also rides, so it is a wonderful way to be together as a family, recreating in nature.

"It feels like we're a normal family," he said. "My adaptive mountain bike gives me the ability to turn down a mountain trail and disappear into the forest, instead of just riding rail and canal trails. There is something very freeing about being outdoors, in the woods, on the trails. To be on my mountain bike in the woods brings great joy to my life." Having the ability and the freedom to mountain bike helps Eric cope with the stress of living with a degenerative disease. Riding with able-bodied people is a huge boost for his self-confidence and happiness.

In Eric's position at a local VA hospital, he often interacts with other veterans. He advocates for adaptive bikes and encourages all the vets in chairs to consider adaptive cycling. He tells them about his brother Chris's foundation and other events where they can try out an adaptive bike. Eric is a powerful example and beacon of hope for these veterans who might not ever learn of the wonderful mobile world of adaptive cycling or the peace that can return to their lives when they enter the forest.

JOHN PACHARIS WAS THIRTY-EIGHT YEARS OLD WHEN HE WAS INVOLVED in an off-road motorbike wreck and suffered a severe knee injury. He was fifteen miles in on a remote trail, got tripped up, fell on his side, and bent the bottom half of his leg ninety degrees to the side, tearing his knee badly. Despite a series of surgeries, he never regained a full range of motion. He sank into a deep depression. You wouldn't know that by talking to or watching John now. He is happy-go-lucky, and has a great sense of humor, laughing and joking with a childlike wonder toward life, and certainly, cycling. "I wasn't always this way," he joked. "Ask my wife. She has seen me at my worst. Sometimes she tells me, 'Get out and go for a bike ride.'"

John experienced post-traumatic stress after the accident, compounded with all the years of being a police officer. John had been a mountain biker most of his adult life. "After my accident, I was not doing well emotionally. I needed to get out of the house and be around other cyclists. I needed to still feel like a cyclist again." He got into adaptive cycling as a way to fight his depression. He learned about BAMBA, Corps Fitness, and the Kaag brothers. John attended BAMBA meetings and borrowed an adaptive handcycle from Chris and the IM ABLE Foundation.

John has some limited use of his legs, so he rides an adaptive recumbent bike, unlike the Kaag brothers, who kneel to cycle. To John, his bike felt like an overbuilt wheelchair with a crank, so he initiated the process of getting an adaptive recumbent mountain bike for himself. A few years after his accident and between his first and second surgeries, John got his own adaptive mountain bike. He has ridden it on every trail in his county.

Today, John puts an impressive fifteen hundred miles a year on his bike. It is his way to vent and his path to happiness. He leads weekly community rides for BAMBA, sharing his love and knowledge of the trails with everyone. Once he realized how much getting into the woods by means of a mountain bike had helped him, he got an idea to create an Adaptive Day with BAMBA in Reading. BAMBA's annual adaptive cycling day introduces as many disabled folks as possible to the world of mountain biking. A variety of adaptive bikes are available to ride, and there are talks and demos throughout the day. "There are different levels of disabilities," John explains. "Some disabled are nervous about being out in the woods. Some feel unsteady when they first begin to ride an adaptive bike and are a little more cautious over the terrain. We are here to help make that experience as easy and fun as possible. We want to show people that they can get out on the trails again, regardless of what challenges life has thrown at you. Exercise is very important for the disabled. It not only builds strength and fitness, but it prevents them from feeling useless. If you don't do things to improve yourself, you can sink into a deep depression."

John is more mobile than the Kaag brothers and could walk out of the woods if he wrecked his bike. Chris Kaag explained how he was riding solo on the mountain one evening and "turtled." Turtling is the term for when a handcycle tips over sideways. The disabled cyclist gets stuck underneath and cannot move. He needs help to unstrap, crawl out from under it, remount, and continue. When it happened to Chris, he called for help on his cell and laid there until they arrived. He promised his family and buddies never to mountain bike solo again.

Pacharis and the Kaag brothers break their adaptive cycles quite often. "If the trail is off-camber, where it comes across a hillside on an angle," explained John, "it doesn't take much to pop that wheel and drop you over."

The trio proves that adaptive cyclists can be out there too, riding the same rugged mountain bike trails, keeping up, and inspiring everyone. They work with BAMBA to make the trails around Berks County and Reading adaptable—building wider trails, cutting blowdowns, and constructing appropriate bridges for the wider adaptive tires. Their goal is to get more disabled folks moving on adaptive bikes. To watch disabled people propel themselves through the woods is nothing short of exciting. Everyone benefits from witnessing a few more miracles in life. As John says, "The bike will set you free."

FELIX (PONCHO) PENA, VIETNAM VETERAN, HEADED OUT ON A MOONLIT night to do some "gravel crunching" on the Schuylkill River Trail, a national heritage greenway that follows the Schuylkill River from the coal regions of Pennsylvania down to Philadelphia, tracing the path of the Industrial Revolution. "I can't jump out of airplanes at night anymore, so I like to cycle at night," he said, "especially when the moon is full." Poncho is viewed as the "badass senior cyclist" in BAMBA, although he would disagree. The younger riders look to him for inspiration. Poncho can easily roll twenty-five miles on the Schuylkill River Trail and sixty miles on his road bike. It is closing in on fifty years since Poncho flew into Vietnam's Cam Ranh Bay as an REMF ("rear echelon motherfucker"), as part of a five-man Ranger team. He did hunter/killer POW missions in the Vietnam boonies, sneaking around and setting up ambushes. He still has residual trauma from the war. Cycling helps him deal with it.

Some nights, flashbacks from the war startle him awake. Very vivid memories of the woods being full of enemies fill his dreams. He hears the words that Eisenhower spoke, "We need young men to send into war," and it causes him to spiral down. He got along with the Vietnamese people, and their abandonment by the US government still weighs heavily on his mind. When he returned home from the war to his little hometown of Laredo, Texas, in 1971, he wasn't greeted with hostility like many veterans around the country. Laredo was one of the poorest towns in America, and many of the Mexican American men from there went into the armed forces after high school. Poncho struggled with rage and guilt for not going back to fight after his time was up. His buddies were still being blown up, mostly by booby traps planted by the Vietcong, but he was home safe. Survivor guilt was very prevalent among veterans after the Vietnam War, as it is among today's veterans of wars in the Middle East. Poncho drank to numb his pain, to self-medicate.

After his nearly three years of active service, Poncho went to under-grad and graduate school, then bounced around looking for the right job until finally settling on a journalism career. Throughout his college years, he cycled to and from the University of Texas at Austin, remembering the freedom he had felt cycling as a youth. Even when he started his journalism career, the six miles he rode every weekday to work, as well as longer rides on weekends, brought him great happiness. As decades passed, Poncho did less and less cycling until 2011 when he retired from his work as a writer and editor. A year or so before that, at a doctor's examination, he discovered that his blood sugar and cholesterol numbers had soared, so his health was a mess. After all these years, with extra time on his hands, his post-traumatic stress from Vietnam reared its ugly head. Images of his buddies dying came back to haunt him, so his use of alcohol returned as a coping mechanism.

"I went through a horrible period. When I don't have other things to occupy my mind, I brood about the past." Poncho tried counseling designed especially for Vietnam veterans, but it didn't feel right to him: "I figured if your thoughts take you to where it hurts, don't go there." Susan Pena, Poncho's wise wife of more than forty years, encouraged him to get back in the saddle. He hooked up with the Berks County Bicycle Club, which takes advantage of the many miles of country roads through farmland and forest. His old bike had worn out, so Poncho bought a hybrid, then a road bike, and, more recently, a mountain bike. He got involved with the local road-bicycling club and then with BAMBA. He related to the Marine vets Chris and Eric Kaag and John Pacharis, and how through BAMBA and their individual efforts, they help the community.

After Poncho helped BAMBA build bridges to allow adaptive cycles to cross the streams, he was inspired to explore the mountain-bike trails himself. "They have some very inspiring cyclists," he said, "but every now and then I run across a whippersnapper who is surprised that I can keep up a brisk pace."

UNLIKE MOST MOUNTAIN-BIKING COMMUNITIES, BAMBA DOES NOT FOCUS on building bigger, more challenging technical trails, which can make the sport intimidating. Getting families, veterans, and disabled folks out enjoying this fun sport is their goal. Giving to the community allows veterans like Chris, Eric, John, and Poncho to heal as they help. Music runs through Poncho's mind as he rides. A rhythm guitarist for most of his life, he moves his pedals to the rhythm in his head.

"When I feel bad," Poncho said, "I go out into nature. The deep woods and mountain paths are especially healing. I love the smells, the sights. After a ride, I feel cleansed. It is one of the best feelings in the world. It gives me a chance to dilute vivid memories of sneaking through the forested mountainside of Vietnam, bent on dealing death to the enemy, and replace them with more recent ones of serenity and joy."

CHAPTER 17

RIVER HOUSE PA VETERANS

RIVER HOUSE PA, MY NONPROFIT that helps veterans heal through outdoor recreation, was started in 2014, soon after Steve Clendenning, Adam Bautz, Tom Gathman, and Stephanie Cutts hiked through my life on the Appalachian Trail. I administered some "trail magic" to them, was deeply moved by their stories, and wanted to do something more. I embraced the challenge of the great right fielder and humanitarian, Roberto Clemente: "Any time we have the opportunity to help someone else and we don't do it, we are wasting our time on earth." When I first considered the idea of helping veterans who have experienced trauma, I was concerned about trust issues. Todd and I do not have military backgrounds, and except for one nephew, we have no relatives in the military. What could we do to make these veterans trust civilians enough to allow us to lead them toward healing in nature?

Before River House partnered with the local VA hospital and medical centers on events, I scheduled my own outings, open to any veteran who suffered from trauma or hard times. One particular veteran, Jesse, had learned about our cycling/paddling outing and emailed, asking to attend. This particular bike ride would take place on a riverside rail trail, followed by a moonlit paddle down the Lehigh River back to the starting point. Jesse had no transportation but really wanted to join in. It made the most sense to have him stay overnight, since the event would end late. I could return him to the VA the next morning. In our emails, he seemed

177

genuine and warm. I offered him the guest cabin, and he secured an over-night pass from the VA. I checked with the VA on his background, and I connected with Jesse on Facebook, where his profile picture showed a big burly Brown man with a barrel chest. He looked like he could have been a wrestler in a previous life.

I loved Jesse as soon as I met him. It felt like I had known him for years. Friendly to everyone in the group—the other vets and their families—he joked around, helped everyone relax and enjoy themselves, and was a very good sport. Nearly everyone paired up in canoes, but Jesse opted to try out a kayak, even though he had never paddled one before. He capsized it, but he took it in stride, happily swimming while the boat was turned upside down and emptied. Jesse's apartment had burned and left him without any material things; he had lost his job and made some poor decisions. Although he was *not* nervous about climbing into a kayak and paddling down a major river for the first time in his life, he *was* apprehensive about spending the night in our guest cabin. He wondered if it was a wise decision on his part, and if he would be safe.

"Think about it," Jesse said. "I don't know you. I'm going to a cabin in the woods, far away. Your husband is a professional chainsaw carver. I could be murdered. I almost bailed." It was laughable, but the military had taught him to always be diligent and prepared. "So I investigated *you*, googled you, watched videos posted about you, and saw that you seemed trustworthy."

I was amazed: he was afraid of Todd and me. Our homeless guest had proved to be one of the most enjoyable houseguests we've ever entertained and, now, a new friend.

HOW DO WE BUILD TRUST AT RIVER HOUSE PA? BY DEMONSTRATING THAT we care about these veterans and have a sincere desire to help. They are hungry to find a better way to live. Our goal is to show them that nature is a place to heal. On a monthly basis, local veterans hospitals and med-ical centers bring vans filled with veterans enrolled in rehab programs for PTSD, substance abuse, homelessness, or all of the above. They are accompanied by their recreational therapists, who believe that recreating in nature can heal.

The nature-based outings are mostly hiking and paddling, but an inner tube down the river, a bike ride on a rail trail, even a yoga class for veterans may round out the events. We make campfires, serve home-cooked meals, and provide a safe space for veterans to experience camaraderie in the beautiful outdoors. Even in the deep of winter, we might go out on owl walks with local birding naturalists, attempting to call in the elusive birds, followed by fun activities like dissecting sterilized owl pellets purchased from a science store. Todd and I have operated River House PA for more than seven years now, and we have made some beautiful friends along the way.

HEADING TO BLUE MARSH LAKE IN BERKS COUNTY TO CANOE AND KAYAK, the vets were pretty pumped, except for a lone young African American man. The rec therapist said that this particular veteran, Lamier, did not want to paddle. He sat apart from everyone else, reading Søren Lynge's *The Seven Principles of Life*. I wondered why the young man had even come. The therapist thought it might be just to get away from the VA. The rehab program tends to be pretty intense.

I walked over to Lamier and knelt down. "You don't think you want to paddle?"

"I'm thinking about it," he said. He had never been in a canoe or kayak before.

There were options, I told him. "You can sit in the front of a canoe and just be a stoker and not be responsible for steering. It's very easy. Plus, it's beautiful out there on the water." Since he'd come all this way, I encouraged him to try it.

Lamier stood up, left his book and his solitary spot on the blanket, and joined the rest of the group at the bank of the lake. Canoe paddling partners had been chosen, and all that remained unspoken for was a solo kayak, which Lamier took. He straggled behind the entire group when we first set off, but he could not wipe the smile off his face. I shared some paddling instructions with him, so he could stroke more efficiently and without fatigue.

Something clicked, and he got the hang of it. Before long, Lamier was out in front, grinning broadly. By the time the paddle was over and we made it back to the bank, Lamier had fallen in love with the sport and was engaging with everyone, talking about what kind of boats are out there and making plans to purchase one of his own someday. Paddling and being on the water could become his personal happy place, where he might find the most peace and healing. A month later, a hike on the Appalachian Trail was on our schedule, which, come to find out, was another first for Lamier. We talked as we hiked together, and he told me a little about his history.

LAMIER HAD BEEN IN THE AIR FORCE FOR THREE YEARS, WORKING AS AN aviation electrician. He grew up in Chester, Pennsylvania, in a peaceful, quiet neighborhood that changed during his youth when the crack epidemic exploded. Dead bodies occasionally popped up in his backyard amid gang violence on the streets. Lamier's mother, a lifer in the military, enforced the rule that her son had to be indoors by the time the street lights came on. Young Lamier's exposure to nature consisted of a lone tree that struggled to live in his backyard. He had seen bald eagles and rivers only on television.

When he was six years old, a classmate of Lamier's wore his Cub Scout vest with its patches to school. He told Lamier about scouting and how they did fun stuff outdoors, but Lamier's mother said no, he could not join. The media had made his mother feel as if the woods were not welcoming nor a safe place for Black people to seek peace. When Lamier was a preteen, his mother was deployed to Sicily, and a neighbor took Lamier on a camping trip to nearby a lake. He fell in love with water and the woods, but filed these feelings away until that day at Blue Marsh and the solo kayak, when he got the opportunity to climb into a boat and power himself across a lake. The three-mile hike was the very first time, at the age of thirty, that Lamier had actually been in the woods. He loved it as much as paddling a kayak across a lake. He loved the peace, the forest, and hiking itself. He had recently experienced therapeutic horseback riding with the VA's rec therapists, and that too had been a powerful first.

There are many historical reasons for the lack of representation in the United States of people of color in the recreational outdoors. For starters, a belief that the forest was off-limits for African Americans during the daylight hours has been passed down for generations. Camille Dungy, professor of English at Colorado State University and editor of *Black Nature: Four Centuries of African American Nature Poetry*, has explored this history. "For many African Americans, the message was clear: parks and wild spaces were off-limits. There are a lot of people who for very valid reasons, can't walk into a grove of trees without feeling terrified." After the African American exodus to America's urban areas in the 1960s, an entirely new generation of Black children had to be taught that the natural world is their home too. When America created the National Park System back in the 1930s, Black people were restricted to their own campgrounds, picnic areas, and comfort stations. Reports of harassment in the national parks continue even today. The Boy Scouts of America did not pass a resolution to integrate until the 1970s.

Organizations like Outdoor Afro, launched in 2009 by Rue Mapp, are attempting to change all that, with the mission statement, "Where Black people and nature meet." The amazing network of eighty outdoor leaders in thirty states has connected thousands of African Americans to the natural world. Outdoor Afro creates a safe place in a variety of outings—from urban nature to the wilderness. The Appalachian Trail Conservancy is also working hard to encourage people of color to use the trail by creating the Next Generation Advisory Council, a group of young, diverse leaders who provide input on policies, campaigns, and strategies.

Michelle Martin, a professor of children and youth services at the University of Washington Information School, trains future librarians in how to best serve young readers. She has documented the huge lack of children's books depicting Black children interacting with nature on any level. "Every reader needs 'mirror stories' to be able to see themselves," she says, which is key to developing empathy. Perhaps if Lamier's mother had had access to books about children of color connecting with nature and recreating outdoors, Lamier might have joined scouting and been on his way much earlier to finding his happy place in the natural world.

The vets took turns speaking around the campfire, sharing what they were grateful for. Lamier said he was grateful for the opportunity to stretch himself and try new things, to be out in nature and to continue living a new life. It was amazing to think that a simple kayak paddle and a walk in the forest can do such good. Some recreational therapists are doing amazing jobs getting veterans outdoors. Besides the important rehab work they do within VA facilities—the meetings, the workshops, the programs—many therapists are beginning to understand how recreating in nature (often called ecotherapy) can heal.

BEFORE WE BEGAN THAT HIKE ALONG THE APPALACHIAN TRAIL, WE stopped in at the Eckville Shelter, the rustic hostel that Todd and I had run under the Volunteers in National Parks Program from 1988 to 1990. Our friend Mick had been running the shelter ever since. We hoped there would be one or two long-distance hikers there, and the vets hiking with us could hear their stories. At the shelter we showed the vets the bunks and the register. A long-distance section hiker cooked up a pot of rice at the picnic table and the guys quizzed him about his life on the trail. Mick shared some stories of running the hostel and how many hikers he serves in a year.

I had fallen in step with one of the veterans, whom I'll call Richard, and he told me his story. In Iraq, he got shot through the gut, which paralyzed his leg (among other things). Richard was in rehab for years until the physical therapist told him to give up and "just accept his new life—in a wheelchair." He would not. Instead, he took two lengths of rope and tied them to the ankle of his paralyzed leg. For nine months, all day long, he pulled it back and forth. He said that he had nothing better to do but to convince his leg to start to move again. Richard's arms got very strong from pulling his leg. He got caught up on watching movies. He said he would just stare at his leg and try to activate his thigh muscle to move, try to make it happen. And then it did, just the tiniest bit. Then Richard knew he would be able to walk again. He practiced balance. He fell a lot. But now, two years later, this inspiring veteran was hiking up and down the Blue Mountain Range, stepping over rocks with ease.

"It taught me not to believe it when someone tells you that you can't do something," Richard said. "It taught me never to give up." Around the campfire, the veterans shared what they are grateful for, what the hike meant to them, and where they are in their lives. "Hiking on the AT has been one of my lifelong dreams," Richard said. "When I got shot, I felt like that dream had been stolen from me. I've been afraid to go out for a hike because I wasn't sure I'd be able to get back. This is the first time I am hiking since before I got shot and it feels really good. I could have been in a wheelchair for the rest of my life, but I'm here and I am so grateful."

Gratitude poured from the veterans' hearts—gratitude for being alive (some have attempted suicide), gratitude for coming to a place of light after so much darkness, gratitude for a second chance, gratitude for the woods and nature and the hike, and gratitude to the rec therapists for believing in nature-based therapy. Some veterans had never been in a forest before or on a hike. They spoke of their renewed desire to climb out of the dark hole, to make wiser, more healthy choices. Tears silently trickled down some of the veterans' cheeks.

Dwelling on gratitude is an amazing healing tool, and neuroscience has revealed that it actually rewires the brain to be happier. Psychologists Robert Emmons of the University of California, Davis, and Michael McCullough of the University of Miami published a study in 2015 that looked at how practicing gratitude affects the physical body. The change takes place in the hypothalamus part of the brain, which is responsible for hormones that regulate emotions. As the hypothalamus is activated by feelings of gratitude, it releases the chemical dopamine, often referred to as "the pleasure hormone." Recalling gratitude over and over in daily life actually rewires the brain so you can evolve into a positive, more compassionate human being.

By the time we are finished with an outing, the vets feel like members of our family, and we invite them back after they graduate from the hospital program. Given the trust issues many of them experience, it is a big deal for them to participate in our programs. But the opportunity to find peace and beauty through these outdoor adventures is pretty important to them. Everyone says their good-byes with a warm hug, a full heart, and the hope that our paths will cross again soon.

WALLY (NOT HIS REAL NAME) IS ANOTHER INCREDIBLE VETERAN WE'VE worked with. He has only one leg but gets around skillfully on crutches. A prosthesis is not an option for this vet, unfortunately, because his hip, where a prosthesis would attach, is also missing. Hiking a mountain trail is a challenge, but Wally wasn't going to let that stop him from trying.

The rec therapists earlier shared that the veterans had requested a hike that was a little more challenging. This particular route had a stream ford with wet, slippery boulders, lots of moss-covered rocks to negotiate, and an incredibly steep, loose, rocky descent on which able-bodied people often slip and fall. The loop hike was well over three miles long. All the vets were young and strong looking. Then I saw Wally step out of the van on his crutches.

I had met Wally before when we paddled at Blue Marsh Lake. His upper body is very strong from hauling his lower body around, but I would question taking some two-legged folks on this hike. I advised the rec therapist to split the group up and take some along a nearby gentle woods road. I would lead the faster, gung ho veterans. But she informed me that everyone decided they wanted to do the more challenging loop, including our vet on crutches. Wow. OK. I was certain that once he got into the rough stuff, he would decide to just enjoy the streamside hike and turn around and meet us at the vans.

We walked along, chatting with the vets as they told me how great it felt to be in the woods. The evening was a beauty—70 degrees, early-fall color highlighting the Appalachian woods, and gorgeous scenery through a hemlock-and-rhododendron forest as the trail paralleled a stream with deep holes and native trout that swam in the shadows. Anyone would be happy in this place but especially veterans involved in a rigorous therapy program. On our hike, one vet told me that he had not been out of his home for two years and stayed indoors away from people and potentially challenging situations, until that evening. He had wrestled with coming or not coming, and finally pushed himself out of his comfort zone and committed. He was extremely happy to be there, and I was happy to share the walk with him.

As my group was finishing the loop and we were approaching the parking lot and the vans, I was looking ahead for our vet on crutches when suddenly my cell phone rang. It was Annie Schnur, a River House board member, who accompanied the "slow" group.

"We are right behind," she said.

"All of you? Even our vet on crutches?" I asked.

"Even him," she replied.

The rest of the vets I had hiked with watched Wally's last steps in amazement. They applauded him as he entered the parking lot, and it was a big moment for all of us. On the hike, Annie overheard many veterans speaking among themselves, about how they were making a change in their lives, how they wanted more—more peace and health and a new life. It was all extremely inspiring, and their handicapped friend's performance made it more so. Just seeing what he did, after many struggled themselves over the same terrain, made them wonder, "If he does not see limits, how can I?"

I don't think our disabled vet knew how big a gift he was giving to all his fellow veterans, and to anyone else who witnessed what he did. There was gratitude in everyone's heart as the long vans pulled away in the night. Their minds were full of conviction—they *can* turn their lives around. Sometimes all it takes is a one-legged rockstar to show you how to do it.

RETIRED MEDIC GILBERT CRUZ-AYALA, WITH THIRTY YEARS IN THE AIR Force and National Guard, has been in a chair for more than a dozen years. He has not walked since he was hit by a mortar at Camp Patriot in Kuwait in 2003. The blast threw him into the air, injuring his back and causing neuropathy of his left leg. On River House activities, Gilbert does not let his lack of mobility hold him back from enjoying nature. His fellow veterans help push his chair down to the lake's edge and lift him into a canoe, so he can paddle as a stoker, or they help push him four miles on a bike trail, up hills and over roots, so he can enjoy the forest.

Gilbert's worst time in the military was when he was working at the medical field hospital in Iraq with the 18th Airborne Division. "Everything changed after that," he recalled. "We were pulling bodies out of helicopters left and right, so many we lost count. Soldiers were committing suicide." Medics have it especially hard. Although they are not the ones actually pulling the trigger and killing, they often suffer massive trauma from witnessing and trying to repair the incredible damage and severity of injuries done to human beings. They have seen broken soldiers, especially the teenagers, coming in scared to death, with limbs blown off. The number of soldiers needing medical treatment had reached into the thousands in a single five-month deployment. A medic might have to deal with treating Iraqi children burned beyond recognition. In accordance with humane war ethics, insurgents could be brought in, blindfolded and handcuffed, needing medical treatment. These people have close-knit, loving families too, and the circumstances that brought them into a conflict are unknown.

Medics only see human suffering, and it is their job, according to both the Geneva convention and the Hippocratic oath, to stop the bleeding, stitch them up, and prevent them from dying. It is very disturbing and confusing for a medic. Some begin to question the motives of war and suffer severe trauma themselves. Gilbert has been in and out of psych wards and at one time attempted suicide. Certain triggers, like sausage browning in a frying pan, bring him right back to burned flesh in Iraq, which paralyzes him. But this Puerto Rican–born nurse goes to the natural world to find peace. He has been connected to nature since his formative years in the Caribbean and then growing up along New York State's Erie Canal.

On his first canoe ride on Landingville Dam in Schuylkill County, Gilbert became mesmerized by the peace and silence. "As soon as Todd told me there was a pair of nesting eagles on the dammed-up river, a mature eagle soared overhead. It was as if he conjured him up. I had never seen such a big, beautiful bird before. It was awesome. Out on the water, I do not feel depressed or anxious. There are no stressors around me. I just feel free. I don't like being in a chair. I don't feel as if I am in charge of my life or my destiny. But on the water, in a boat, I am free." Gilbert wants to get boats for his own family and get back to feeling young and carefree again. He knows that being locked up inside a house is not good for him.

It has been very good for the able-bodied veterans to observe these physically challenged veterans working extra hard to get into nature. They are happy to assist, to share good times on the trail or in the water. It compounds their own personal joy exponentially. Being of service to others can help them heal from their own trauma. For example, another veteran friend, Adam, was gifted a used Prius, which enables him to visit his young son and to pay it forward with fellow veterans. He added an equipment rack to the roof of the car, and he rounds up other veterans multiple times a week and takes them fishing, mountain biking, hiking, even paddling.

He coordinates the outings, acting as both a chauffeur and a cheerleader to get his military brothers who are hurting out moving around in nature. Even while in pain and working through his own trauma, Adam knows that helping others adds to his personal strength while giving strength to his fellow veterans.

VIETNAM VET MIKE SCHNUR WAS ON RIVER HOUSE'S BOARD OF DIRECTORS for many years. As a two-tour veteran of Vietnam with the 173rd Airborne Brigade and the 82nd Airborne Division (1966–1968), he said, "I understand some of what our current generation of combat veterans are working through in their reentry into the 'normal world.'" Currently the commander of VFW Post 12099 based in Allentown, Pennsylvania, Mike plays an active role at River House serving others while facilitating his own healing.

When Mike was a junior in high school, he and his friends blew up toilets with an M-80. The plan was to flush a quarter stick of dynamite, which would create the very cool effect of blowing toilet juice up and out of it, covering the ceiling. But the bomb exploded in the toilet itself, not down in the plumbing, leveling the commode to the floor and embedding chunks of porcelain in the bathroom's ceiling. The boys had hoped for a big effect but nothing quite so spectacular. Mike got in trouble. The disciplinarian wanted to expel him for a year, and after going to court and receiving six months probation, he was told he would need to repeat the eleventh grade. In Mike's mind, that wasn't happening, so he enlisted in the Army and landed in the 82nd Airborne 1st Battalion.

Jumping out of airplanes was even cooler than blowing up toilets. But the love of blowing things up stuck with him, and he got to make that happen again and again in Vietnam. Even though Mike was a rifleman, he always carried grenades in his personal stash because he liked to throw them. "The Vietcong couldn't see the flash of my rifle that way." Mike proudly wears his "173nd Airborne Brigade" baseball cap when the vets from the VA come over for a River House event. The hat is a conversation starter—the vets can see that he is one of them. Over the years Mike has been on the board and helping out at events, he still needs to be prodded occasionally to attend. Like many combat veterans, Mike is sometimes more comfortable staying in his own home and not engaging, even if it's with his fellow band of brothers.

With a bum leg and wanting to put off an unpleasant surgery, Mike usually does not accompany us on our hikes, or at least not very far. Instead, he tends the campfire, ensuring the blaze is warm and high when the group returns for dinner. He keeps the older veterans company who might not be able to hike. Mike has had to learn to extend himself to the vets. Annie, Mike's wife of fifty years, has to nudge him. "Mike has always been a drinker," Annie says, and after he retired from twenty-five years of successfully running his own drywall business, the night drinking escalated into day drinking and the occasional binge drinking. Annie was busy driving a school bus and couldn't stay home to be with her husband. She finally pressed him into getting help. Asking for or accepting help is a hard thing for many older veterans.

Mike, who is ornery and fun-loving, listens to the veterans as they take their turns around the campfire, sharing their stories. It is good for this seventy-year-old Vietnam veteran to hear how this new generation is working to alleviate their trauma and stress. It is not something to hide or be ashamed of. The first step to healing is admitting that you need help, and that is a very hard thing for Vietnam veterans to do. Baring their souls wasn't part of their culture. A bottle of Jack could squelch those sad feelings of losing comrades and killing human beings, events and actions that may still haunt them fifty years later. Other Vietnam vets on River House outings have been self-medicating for decades, and for whatever reason, they have hit such a low spot that they finally seek help. The stigma associated with mental illness and PTSD is very slowly being removed.

Mike has watched the VA vets evolve, grow, and heal. They begin as inpatients in a multimonth rehab program. They can cycle into living in transitional housing at the VA medical facility and score a job on the VA campus and attend River House outings. They can attend events as outpatients, signing up for events in the activities center. Some veterans have attended River House events for many years. We can track their progress as they become happier, more peaceful, and make positive change in their lives. Occasionally, a vet will return to the program, because he backslid and needs more help to get back on track. Observing the vets moving forward, as well as a few backsliding, Mike sees that he is not alone. He *can* do something to help, just by being there with his hat, lighting their fire to provide some warmth and light, standing by as quiet support from another era.

Mike might not know it, but volunteering is one of the best ways to bolster your own personal mental health. Human beings feel good when we help others. Making social connections staves off feelings of loneliness and depression. A study at the Carnegie Mellon University published in *Psychology and Aging* found that volunteering to help others actually lowers blood pressure, reduces stress (which is directly related to health), and decreases mortality risk. Keeping Mike involved ensures that he sticks around longer.

OUR WORK AT RIVER HOUSE USUALLY REVOLVES AROUND HIKING AND PAD-dling, but when my dairy-farmer friends DJ and Loretta Duncan of Robesonia, Pennsylvania, offered the veterans a free experience at their corn maze, I took it. After hosting our veteran friend Dan Stein for a dinner and snowmobile outing one winter evening, they wanted to help more veterans. I hoped the vets wouldn't think going to a corn maze was juvenile. An afternoon and evening at one of the loveliest dairy farms in Berks County doing fun things in the outdoors could be a great release from their rigorous rehab programs at the VA medical center.

As soon as the vans pulled up, the vets tumbled out with outstretched arms, seeking warm embraces; even the ones meeting me for the first time. Most of them were men. They must have been clued in on the drive over about this Sicilian nonprofit director who loves to hug. They just knew it felt good, but I know how important it is to their healing. Psychologist Virginia Satir said, "There is a great deal of scientific evidence proving the importance of hugging and physical contact." Here are a few of the benefits:

- Hugging stimulates oxytocin, a neurotransmitter that creates feelings of contentment while reducing stress and anxiety.
- Hugging stimulates the thymus gland, which is located at the base of the sternum. This important gland regulates and balances our white blood cell level, which has the important job of fighting disease.

- Hugging releases endorphins and serotonin into the blood, chemicals that are responsible for making us feel happy while negating sadness and pain.
- Hugging balances the nervous system, when the tiny pressure centers located on the skin called Pacinian corpuscles are stimulated. They send messages to the vagus nerve in the brain in the form of electric impulses, which creates balance in the body.
- Finally, according to new research out of the University of California, hugging makes men more affectionate, better at forming relationships and social bonding.

AFTER WELCOMING EMBRACES, THE VETS GOT A RUN-DOWN OF THE DAY'S activities: there was a corn maze exploration; gourd-chucking with giant slingshots aimed at toilet bowls and other metal contraptions in the field; sliding down the insides of black ribbed irrigation tubes; a hay ride around the bucolic farm; a farm tour to the milking parlor to see how cows are automatically milked; meeting freshly born calves and bottle-feeding them; and preparing (Paul) Bunyan burgers cooked over charcoal. For the night's grand finale, we ignited colored-paper Chinese lanterns, watched them swell with hot air, and released them into the sky.

As soon as the guys spotted the slingshots, they were off. Something to shoot! Loretta gave them buckets to go into the fields and gather gourds. One came back with a huge neck pumpkin. "Not that!" she informed them. "That's to make pumpkin pie with." But they would have shot anything. They behaved like little kids, cheering each other's accomplishments when their gourds hit a bull's-eye. After sliding down the irrigation tubes, they paired off to ride the seesaws, which I am sure they hadn't done for decades. There was so much happy laughter echoing around the fields. Loretta finally pulled them away from the shooter and gave them their cue sheets to help them navigate the many turns inside the corn maze. The first one out won. They ran off in teams, helping one another, playing and giggling in the sunlight like youngsters. I stood atop the elevated stairs in the maze and happily watched them. No one was thinking about therapy or rehab, yet that is exactly what they were doing, returning to a simpler, happier time before drugs, alcohol, and depression.

Adults move away from play very quickly as they leave their childhood behind, but according to an article by Lawrence Robinson, Melinda Smith, Jeanne Segal, and Jennifer Shubin in *Harvard Health Publication HelpGuide*, "The Benefits of Play for Adults," as well as several other studies, play is still very important. It adds much-needed laughter and pure joy to adults' overly serious lives (which veterans in rehab certainly have). These are medicines for the soul; childlike play and laughing are great sources of relaxation, stress reducers, and connectors to others. Engaging in laughter and play fosters a positive, optimistic outlook on life and reduces aggression. Anthony T. DeBenedet, M.D., author of *Playful Intelligence: The Power of Living Lightly in a Serious World*, writes: "Humor is also one of our strongest forces of resiliency. It can give us a little air when we can barely catch our breath. Humor does this by moving us psychologically, ever-so-slightly away from the stressors that we are facing. Having or exploring these moments of humor doesn't mean that we're trying to avoid or escape what's in front of us; it just means that we are using our playful intelligence to lighten our suffering."

After the vets surfaced from the maze, River House board member Tim Minnich taught them how to assemble and build their foil-wrapped Bunyan burgers. They began with a huge patty of ground beef and then selected ingredients including sliced potatoes, carrots, celery, onions, peppers and a wide range of gravy and sauce mixes to add into a foil packet, along with a little water. While they cooked and steamed over a charcoal fire, the vets went back to more playing. When Tim announced the burgers were cooked, the vets slowly unwrapped the packages, allowing the steam and the delicious aromas to escape. No one could believe how incredibly delicious they were and that they had made them themselves.

I met Tim years ago when on assignment with *Scouting* magazine. His Venture crew of teens had just completed the 100 Mile Wilderness in Maine on the Appalachian Trail, and I was to write a feature story on their adventure. My children and I climbed Mount Katahdin, the trail's northern terminus, with them all and thus began a lifelong friendship. Tim was well versed on leading groups in outdoor excursions and loved to cook. His big heart embraced the vets in our program, and his meals of smoked-barbecue ribs, shrimp boils, homemade French fries, and hand-cranked ice cream are legendary. Tim has the vets coming back for more, and eating his food probably ranks right up there with the fun of recreating out in nature.

After dinner, the tractor towing a hay wagon came down, and the vets climbed on, making themselves comfortable on the hay bales. We traveled across the fields to the milking parlor where they saw how the cows are ushered in, their teats cleaned and disinfected, the suction tubes attached, and the milk extracted. The cows are so big, and slightly intimidating if you are a city boy, which some of the vets are, but they learned where our milk comes from and saw the actual process of extracting it. They asked a ton of questions about the workload, milk quantity, how much the cows eat, their schedule, how long they live, and on and on. The vets were truly fascinated and excited to learn. After the milk parlor, we went over to the calf barn, where the vets were surprised how desperately the young things wanted to suck on their fingers, as many were newborns and had the uncontrollable desire to nurse. A few of the vets jumped right into the pens, bottle-fed and bonded with the babies, some even talking to them in soft voices like cow whisperers.

Back at the campfire, I took out my brightly colored Chinese paper lanterns, opened them up, inserted the fuel squares, and lit them. The vets gently held the lanterns open and helped them expand, working in teams. They could see the colored tissue paper swelling from the hot air inside and could feel the lanterns wanting to go, up, into the heavens. With soft fingertips, they released them. We threw our heads back and watched them climb higher and higher—bright, glowing, colored orbs floating and gently rocking with the stars.

Before the vets went back to the medical center, their rec therapists had them go around the campfire and share what this event had meant to them. Many vets admitted to having had a very hard week, as they were challenged and felt down, but some of that dissipated here at the farm. The rec therapists said that it did even *their* hearts good to hear so many of the vets laughing. One veteran said, "I so enjoyed being a kid again. I realized that I could be and I should be doing these kinds of things with my own son." Some of the vets said they had experienced up to six firsts in their life there at Duncan's Farm. One said that it had truly been "the best day of his life," and he had already lived through four decades. Who would have thought a corn maze could do so much?

"When I released that sky lantern tonight," one veteran said, "I felt a real release inside of me, a lifting up, a letting go of my past life." Another said, "I was reminded today that there is a whole other life out here for me—sober and healthy."

EPILOGUE

WALKING TOWARD PEACE IS NOT about where these veterans started out, how damaged or broken they became. It is about the progress they have made and where each one is today in their journey of healing. They have courageously shared their personal experiences, because they were able to begin to move beyond them. The following updates on many of the profiled veterans are presented in the order they appeared in these pages.

STEVE CLENDENNING

Shortly after Steve finished his Appalachian Trail thru-hike, he and his wife, Ruby, moved away from the Marine base in Camp Lejeune, South Carolina, where Ruby had worked as a federal employee. Their intention was to distance themselves from the Marines and transition to their own personal identities. The couple bought a house close to the Appalachian Trail in Martinsburg, West Virginia, so Steve could access the beloved trail whenever he desired. He got himself a black Lab, Maggie, who is enrolled with Steve in classes to become his service dog. "She's my little angel," Steve says.

The couple has two more angels in their lives—their son, Sean, who is now five, who keeps Steve busy and very happy, and the newest addition, Carlee, who was born in March 2020. Since Ruby works at the US Department of Veterans Affairs, Steve is in charge of all the household chores, looking after the baby, preparing dinner, taking his son to school, paying the bills, and keeping up with appointments. Every year Steve and Ruby pick up veterans who are walking off their war on the Appalachian Trail. Steve "feeds and waters them" and slack-packs them for days. He has given up drinking completely and is off all his meds too, making him a little more emotional in life, but he likes himself better this way. "I'm real. This is me," he says. "I might never get back to the Steve I once was, but I am trying and I want to get as close as I can get."

ADAM BAUTZ

Adam's trail-hiking guide company, Outdoor Travel Tours, is rated as the number-one hiking experience in the Las Vegas area on Tripadvisor. A highlight in his years of leading hundreds of clients into the beautiful desert was a physically challenged client in a wheelchair. The chair was no obstacle to Adam's desire to connect the young man with the natural world, even if it meant carrying him in his arms. "This was one of the most rewarding experiences of my life," Adam said.

TOM GATHMAN

Today Tom is a paid athlete working for Mountainsmith, an outdoor-gear manufacturer. He designs, tests, and endorses their gear, collecting royalties afterward. Although he does not need a lot of money to be happy, Tom hopes to establish himself in the outdoor industry and to be financially secure. Many veterans have PTSD, and some suffer from physical disabilities, like Tom, who has chronic pain from years of abuse to his body. Yet he manages it, and hiking alleviates much of that pain.

To date, Tom has hiked between twenty and twenty-five thousand miles. His long trail experiences have taken him across the ocean to foreign countries. The Jordan Tourism Board brought him over to the Middle East as part of an international team of backpackers to traverse the 404-mile Jordan Trail, established in 2015, that travels the length of the country. As a neighbor of Iraq, Jordan was the closest Tom has come to the war zone since his last deployment, and the trip was the first time he had returned to the Middle East. It was a positive experience, and it opened up a whole new world for him. Kenya and Rwanda are looking into establishing long-distance hiking trails across their countries and are considering hiring Tom as a consultant.

ILENE HENDERSON

Since Ilene began her new life as National Park Ranger, she admits that "it has not all been smooth 'hiking' thus far. I have had a lot of 'rocks and roots' along the way. On the AT, there are a few sections that are known to not be blazed or not blazed well; but compared to the challenges on the trail of life, I enjoy the challenge and trudge onward!"

Ilene is remodeling a third motor home, a 1993 Dutchmen Royal, which she and her mother, Inga, will live in. "My mom jokes that I should go into the RV renovation business, but I will stick to being a park ranger for now." Ilene is now working with the National Forest Service in the San Juan and Uncompahgre National Forests near Montrose, Colorado. She is an Off-Highway Vehicle Forest Ranger doing trail maintenance. She also patrols and checks that visitors are observing the rules. She rides four-wheelers, ATVs, and UTVs (utility task/terrain vehicle)—a machine-loving girl's dream.

TOMMY BUCCI

Tommy has struggled with suicides and overdoses among veteran friends, which has left him feeling numb. These tragedies have fueled his desire to reach out and help more veterans. "I will continue to do trips with these guys until I am dead," he said. In 2019 he tallied up 123 events with his nonprofit, Soldier Sanctuary, including 585 total hours for Tommy and 242 hours for his therapy dogs. His plans for the future? "I hope to retire fully in 2026, and then . . . well, there are a lot of ladies out there who might require my attention. I'll probably adopt more retired military working dogs, live in a shack by a river, fade away, and regroup in hell with the rest of the Airborne."

MARIO KOVACH

After Mario's retirement, the Kovachs moved to the family farm on 163 acres in Upstate New York. His service dog, Bunker, helped him with the transition from military service to civilian life. After three years as Mario's service dog, Bunker does not need to perform in that role any-more, because Mario is moving forward. Now Bunker is just enjoying the sweet life as a pet.

Mario studied animal behavior and conservation at a local university to become a better dog handler. He would like to play an active role in a nonprofit that helps and protects people in some way. He believes he would be a natural at it after so many years of working to keep people safe. Mario feels obligated to help others and firmly believes in the concept of fostering post-traumatic growth. Dog-training and dog-obedience schools is where he'll begin, teaching dog owners how to communicate, and then branching into work with service dogs. Mario is looking into starting his own school. "It's time for me to journey on," he shared. "Time to analyze myself, proceed at my own pace, not worry about anyone else, gift myself the time to spend inside my own head, learn what my strengths and weaknesses are, and begin to like myself again."

SHAWN MURPHY

Shawn left the LF Ranch in 2018 and moved to the Seattle area, seeking a better paying job so that he could be closer to his daughter, Audrey. He dislikes city life, though, because it's difficult for him to maintain serenity, and he misses the ranch and being outdoors. "But this is where Audrey is, and I am jazzed by how close we have become. For me, this is why I made myself better. My addiction hurt her and affected her life. She understands what happened and doesn't hold it against me. With my daughter, there is no wall. I am me without any filter. Audrey and I have much in common and we understand each other. She understands my past, my errors, my lifestyle. When I look at Audrey, I truly see her; she is part of me and yet she is herself. She is the closest I am to any human."

This says a whole lot about Audrey, who was willing and able to turn the page on past decades and move forward with her father, in joy and with hope. "My whole life, I thought I was unwanted by my father," she said. "Now I know he was only trying to protect me from his addiction. I'm proud of him and how he fought the demons off." The pair discovers new things every time they are together.

Shawn witnessed the marriage of his daughter to her best friend, Gagan. "It was one of those times when your feelings run deeper than mere words," he said. "Now if she would just do her part and have a child!" Shawn said. "I am looking forward to having a little one to share nature with." In the near future, Shawn plans to hike the 500-mile Finger Lakes Trail in New York with "my hiking buddy, Zelda, the dog I had on the LF Ranch. Zelda is the one who keeps me sane. On the ranch I learned that nature and animals are the only medications I need."

STEPHANIE CUTTS

Today Steph lives in South Carolina and works at a flower shop, where every single day she is surrounded in beauty. She helps people by sending love in the form of beautiful flowers, which directly impacts her life positively. This is very important to Steph, because in 2018, she suffered the greatest loss of her life—the death of her beloved, Frank, who was involved in a motorcycle accident. He collided with a car on the freeway and died at the scene. Hiking the Appalachian Trail a half dozen years before Frank's tragic accident taught Steph about strength, how to dig in and never give up, especially on a tough day. The healing and personal growth she experienced on the AT enabled her to appropriately grieve and navigate the trauma of losing Frank. She wrote about it extensively and is working through all the emotions involved, so that she can heal and not experience post-traumatic stress.

Being proactive about her healing, Steph learned of a nonprofit called Uuzilo, whose mission is to help those who have experienced a sudden, traumatic, and unexpected life-altering event resulting in PTSD or profound grief. They take participants to Africa for eight weeks, where they embark on an intimate, extended motorcycle expedition. Uuzilo provides the BMW motorcycles, safety equipment, and camping gear, as well as leadership, while the participants work on recovering from their trauma. Steph was the perfect candidate—an experienced rider, suffering from grief, and a motorcycle mechanic and long-distance backpacker—so she was used to rough conditions. "The adventure was exactly what I needed," she said, "but it was also the scariest thing I have ever done. I had to dig so far into myself because there was no giving up. We were in the middle of nowhere and I had to figure everything out. No one could ride the motorcycle but me. I did it to honor Frank and his love for riding."

Hiking is still Steph's go-to place to become happy and experience peace. "The trail taught me that outdoor therapy works, that I could walk off my fears and doubts, and let go of my burdens." Now, when the loss of Frank gets too much for Steph, she says, "I just take a hike and let nature soothe my aching soul. Nature holds me close, lets my thoughts and words flow in my mind, until I can make sense of it all again."

TRAVIS JOHNSTON

Travis still struggles with the events that took place on that fateful day in the Afghan mountains. "Discussing it is painful and I relive it almost daily," he says. "Some days I hurt more than others; some days those memories are absent, yet sometimes they seem to occupy every corner of my brain. I've accepted that I will deal with this the rest of my life, but I am determined to improve and work on forgiving myself and others. I can't change the past. The present and future are priority. I want to always be getting healthier and sustain my perpetual improvement."

Travis is working toward becoming certified as a flight paramedic, a hazmat (hazardous materials) technician, and eventually completing a bridge program to become a registered nurse. He has successfully completed his fire training at the Alabama Fire College. He graduated as valedictorian, received the Academic Excellence Award, and won the peer vote for the Class Leadership Award. He is currently working with Daufuskie Island Fire Department in South Carolina. He refuses to give up his love of travel, so he aims to work for the Department of Defense after he completes the rest of his training, which will enable him to work with Federal Emergency Services anywhere in the world where the United States has a base, which is nearly everywhere. He's decided that hiking is an integral part of his life and plans to continue seeking trails wherever he lives. Travis and Kaya married. He hopes to own a farm, grow his own food, and keep animals.

SEAN REILLY

Sean married his Abu Daubi sweetheart, Carly, who hails from Calgary, Alberta, Canada. They moved to Calgary, where they receive much support from her loving extended family. The couple brought a beautiful baby girl into the world named Jordyn. "Since having our daughter," Carly reports, "I have never seen Sean so truly happy. You can see how full his heart is. It is hard to put into words what a good father he is. It's as if this was what he was meant to do." Carly says Sean is constantly playing with Jordyn, laughing with her, bouncing her on his shoulders. Jordyn turns to Sean when she cries. "They both light up a room when they see each other."

However, there is still military trauma. He still wakes up at night and screams. "The bads can be bad but the goods are so good," she says. "In addition to being a wonderful father, he is such a good husband, brother, son, and friend." Sean currently works as a health and safety representative in the oil and gas industry. "We laugh a lot in our simple, full-of-love life," says Carly. Sean agrees: "I love being a dad—best job ever. I could never believe I could love someone so much. I am so blessed to have my family." To get himself out into the natural world more often, Sean has taken up fishing. The family was blessed with a baby boy in the fall of 2020.

DAN STEIN

In Colorado, Dan finally received relief from his chronic pain when he learned about craniosacral therapy. "When my all-consuming physical pain finally subsided, and I wasn't in misery twenty-four seven," he said, "I was then forced to look at my emotional pain." His addiction to alcohol continued to control him.

Dan learned about an intensive two-week rehab program in Boston, Massachusetts, run by the Wounded Warrior Program, and what a miracle it proved to be for him. For two weeks, he was in sessions with a small group of a half-dozen other veterans. No drugs or alcohol were allowed, and Dan acquired terrific tools to help him cope. He feels like he is finally learning how to live again. "I think about how I used to be and I don't want to be like that anymore. I've had enough of that destructive way of living." In Boston, with a clear head, he began to remember what occurred during the war. He was finally able to talk about the pain and suffering in a safe place with other veterans.

Dan fathered a son and decided to move back East, where his mother lives, so he could play a role in his son's life. He returned to Reading, Pennsylvania, and bought a house in the country. He is remodeling his home, planting a big garden, rock climbing, and hiking, and he is now a board member of the nonprofit, River House PA. "I have forgiven myself for my bad decisions," he says. That in itself is spectacular progress.

JESSE BIER

Jesse moved to Idaho to be near his biological father and other family members. He currently works at an auto parts store, helping folks in this field where he has much knowledge. Another long-distance hike is in his future, but he has since shifted his sights to the Continental Divide Trail. Service dog extraordinaire Cooper will surely accompany him.

GABE VASQUEZ

In 2020, while he waited for the summer to begin in America, Gabe hiked across New Zealand during their summer. He also hiked the 500-mile Camino de Santiago (The Way of Saint James), a pilgrim path in Spain. Gabe's plans for the summer of 2020 were to paddle the Missouri River, 3,500 miles from its source in Montana to the Gulf, which would be his eighth crossing of America. Gabe has already covered 16,200 miles of his 23,000-mile Cross America expeditions, which he hopes to finish in 2021. He feels more peaceful with every hike.

GILBERT CRUZ

In 2019, Gilbert enrolled in a nineteen-day intensive chronic pain rehabilitation therapy program at the James A. Haley VA Medical Center in Tampa, Florida. The program seeks to improve the quality of life by treating chronic pain holistically. Gilbert learned exercises, skills, and techniques to "make his life bigger," as Dr. Nicolle Angeli, the inpatient clinical director, put it, "so pain relatively feels smaller and more manageable." Gilbert enjoyed heated-pool therapy, relaxation training, educational classes, recreation therapy, physical therapy, walking for exercise, yoga, tai chi, and virtual reality and biofeedback sessions.

Gilbert had a bulging disc and had to undergo laser surgery to relieve the pain on his spinal cord. After he recuperated, it was back to more med-free, holistic therapy. He happily walked out of the medical center with the help of a walker, leaving the wheelchair behind. Getting back on the trail and securing his own kayak are the immediate goals in Gilbert's more mobile future.

AUTHOR'S NOTE:
THE PATH TO HEALING AND POST-TRAUMATIC GROWTH

IN CREATING THIS BOOK, I acted merely as a conduit, streaming the veterans' stories through me like electricity. I was their storyteller. I was their voice. Although their experiences with pain and trauma broke my heart, I also found great joy while working on this project. I came to feel like each and every one of these veterans, no matter their age, were my kids and I was their mother, loving them unconditionally. My life has been blessed by knowing them.

The most important point these veterans want to get across is not where they may have started out, but where they are today and how their experiences in the outdoors have helped them. That is why they have shared their darkest and deepest personal feelings, because they were able to move through and beyond them, and the healing continues as time goes on. Walking, the sport of choice for most of the veterans profiled in this book, was chosen because it is the one that I too am most familiar with. The activity of walking is accessible for the masses. But there are many other sports and ways to access the natural world: mountain climbing, rafting, horseback riding, fishing, scuba diving, and more. There are many organizations that offer adventure trips for veterans, and all of these programs have in common a belief in nature healing and have enjoyed tremendous success in helping to heal struggling veterans. (You'll find some of these organizations in the appendix at the end of this book). Each veteran should explore as many ways as he or she is able to discover the path to healing that speaks most to the heart, and participate in that activity as frequently as possible.

At the time of this writing, a bipartisan-supported bill called the Accelerating Veterans Recovery Outdoor Act, H.R. 2435/S.1263, 116th Cong. (2019), sponsored by Representatives Chris Smith (R-NJ) and Adam Smith (D-WA), is gaining interest in Congress. The bill, if enacted, would require the Secretary of Veterans Affairs to establish an interagency task force on the use of public lands to provide medical treatment and ecotherapy to veterans through outdoor recreation. While that bill remains in committee, in November 2020 the Department of the Interior announced that veterans would be granted free access to all national parks, wildlife refuges, and other federal lands. These spaces can offer veterans and their families places of historical connection (of 419 National Park sites, 156 commemorate and interpret America's military history). In addition to providing historical connection, national parks and other public lands offer veterans and their families solace and recreation, where they can heal together and create shared memories.

The Department of Veterans Affairs is getting involved in ecotherapy. In 2016, on the grounds of Walter Reed National Military Medical Center in Bethesda, Maryland, the therapeutic nature space known as The Green Road was constructed. Designed by Harvard scientists, this green space is the first of its kind, used to conduct research on what happens when veterans suffering with PTSD come in direct contact with the elements of nature. There is an increasing belief that something other than, or at least in addition to, medication is needed for healing. The philosophy of The Green Road Project Administrator and retired Navy physician, Captain Fred Fotte, is that "nature itself is both sacred and healing. It has the sacred qualities of boundlessness, intimacy, and transcendence, and the idea of what we are doing is sacred as well as useful and fun. Your body feels better, your mind and imagination work because you see a wider world and you want to be part of it."

All of the veterans profiled in *Walking Toward Peace* know these things intimately. Their stories are, as my friend Army Ranger Travis Johnson put it, "a microcosm of what our lives are like a lot of the time: Unorganized. Sad. Manic. Unsure. Disarrayed. Bipolar. Driven yet random. Filled with intent yet continually falling short of others' and our own standards. Guilt-ridden pride. Confusing emotional discourse." Coauthors Ken Falke and Josh Goldberg, who wrote about post-traumatic growth in their book *Struggle Well: Thriving in the Aftermath of Trauma,* have explained that, "Sharing your story is a key step in moving beyond some of the harmful by-products of struggle—like depression, anxiety, and PTSD. It's what we choose to learn from our struggle that matters. You can choose to *react* negatively, or you can choose to *respond* positively, turning your struggle into strength." The veterans profiled here chose post-traumatic growth as their compass bearing. They literally walked the trail from struggle to strength. These journeys show that healing from PTSD is possible and that those in pain can create a new normal in their lives. Extended time in the natural world can play a significant role; longer and more often is better but short bursts in nature are also very good.

Now that you know a little more about the emotional turmoil some veterans harbor and the burdens they carry, may you be encouraged to go out into your own community and extend a helping hand to your local veterans, to lighten their load. May we as humans strive to end war and find a way to seek peace first, for the costs and consequences these veterans bear is lifelong. May we always remember the Mother we have in the natural world and go there any time we need peace and healing.

ACKNOWLEDGMENTS

I WOULD LIKE TO THANK my wonderful husband, Todd Gladfelter, a chainsaw carving artist who happily and untiringly supported my ass while I wrote this book. Becoming obsessed with a project is necessary if an author is to do a good job on a book, so I did little else during the process and was a kept woman for multiple years. It will even out, Dear Husband, I promise.

My son, Bryce Gladfelter, did an amazing job illustrating the veterans. I am hugely grateful for these portraits. His heart and soul went into each face as he studied every personal story and got to know each veteran intimately. Their brilliance shines through because of his brilliance as an artist. This work was an act of love on his part. I am eternally grateful. I hope your life, like mine, has been made more beautiful from this work.

I would like to thank my friends who read the manuscript and offered me their ideas and expertise, especially Lynne Williams, clinical psychologist, who added her knowledge and wisdom and so generously allowed me to insert it seamlessly throughout the book. Lynne has much experience working with PTSD among veterans, both in her clinical private practice and in the prison system. I appreciate not needing to go back to school to earn a psych degree, Lynne. Also, my thanks go to Chief Petty Officer US Navy (Ret.) Michael Foy, who has more than fourteen years experience managing US Army Outdoor Recreation Services and Programs in California and Georgia, and is also a skilled editor. Mike reviewed the manuscript for accuracy and clarity, especially pertaining to military language and culture. Great friend, writer, and editor, Maryalice Yakutchik, also reviewed the manuscript to make sure I sounded authentic and authoritative to my readers.

I would like to thank my editor, Kate Rogers, from Mountaineers Books, who has been with me for decades, through multiple books, always believing in the ideas I had to share. I appreciate you. My developmental editor, Amy Smith Bell, who made the manuscript flow and make sense with as much love and sensitivity as if it were her own words, and copy editor, Ellen Wheat, who did a great job cleaning up the text. Thank you.

But most important, I want to thank the veterans who so courageously opened their hearts and not only let me in, but allowed all of my readers in, too. Their trust in me is deeply moving and appreciated. There could be no book without their stories, and there would be no hope without their experiences walking toward peace on the trail to wisdom.

APPENDIX:
PROGRAMS THAT TAKE VETERANS INTO NATURE

THIS LIST REPRESENTS ONLY A smattering of the programs that take veterans into nature across the country. In Pennsylvania alone, there are a few hundred nonprofits offering services to veterans, many of them nature based. Some of these include Pennsylvania Outdoor Veterans, Wounded Warrior Patrol (skiing and snowboarding for veterans and their families), LEEK (hunting), and my own, River House PA. Some VA facilities employ recreational therapists who believe in ecotherapy and offer outings for inpatient as well as outpatient nature-based excursions. Encourage your local VA to explore alternative possibilities in your area and create partnerships with organizations that work to connect folks to the natural world, to assist in healing.

Higher Ground
https://highergroundusa.org
This organization offers adaptive sports and therapeutic recreation programs, and experiential programs incorporating structured activities.

National Outdoor Leadership School (NOLS)

www.nols.edu/military

Wyoming-based expedition or wilderness medicine training, EMT training, and career-focused outdoor education courses. NOLS is the leader in wilderness education, providing awe-inspiring, transformative experiences. Students can use the Post-9/11 GI Bill for nondegree programs. These offerings are gateways to new careers, exploration, and personal growth.

Northeast Passage

www.nepassage.org

This nonprofit offers recreational therapy services that support the health and well-being of individuals with a variety of disabilities and health issues. A nonprofit affiliated with the University of New Hampshire (fifty miles north of Boston), it provides innovative solutions for children, adults, and military veterans with disabilities.

Operation Purple Healing Adventures

www.militaryfamily.org/programs/operation-purple/healing-adventures/

This free three-day experience run by the National Military Family Association combines family-focused activities with outdoor exploration, like hiking and canoeing, to encourage each family's growth on their new journey post injury.

Outdoor Buddies

https://outdoorbuddies.org

This nonprofit offers a variety of outdoor Colorado-based programs for mobility-disabled individuals, veterans, and youth.

Outward Bound

www.outwardbound.org/veteran-adventures

Backpacking, mountaineering, climbing, canoeing, sailing, kayaking, whitewater rafting, and dog sledding. Outward Bound for Veterans helps returning service members and recent veterans readjust to life at home through powerful wilderness courses that draw on the healing benefits of teamwork and challenge through the use of the natural world. Positive emotional and mental outcomes are the goal.

Project Healing Waters

https://projecthealingwaters.org
Dedicated to the physical and emotional rehabilitation of disabled active military service personnel and disabled veterans through fly fishing and associated activities including education and outings.

Project Sanctuary

www.projectsanctuary.us
Helps the military family as a unit. Therapeutic retreats in eight states with certified recreational therapists.

Remedy Alpine

www.remedyalpine.org
"Work the mountain—rest your mind." This Alaska-based organization has one single goal, which is to share their passion for the outdoors with our veteran community and share the healing experience the outdoors creates within each of us. Remedy Alpine provides half-day, full-day, and multiday outdoor adventures for military and veterans with a simple goal: to heal the mind and spirit.

Ride 2 Recovery

https://weareprojecthero.org/events/challenges
A groundbreaking veterans program that saves lives by restoring hope and purpose. The Challenge Series is an incredible event that brings together injured veterans, active military, and public supporters in a multiday journey that covers hundreds of miles and is a once-in-a-lifetime experience. This organization was founded on cycling-based programs—the Honor Ride Series. The Honor Ride Series is made up of one-day community events geared toward raising awareness and funding for Ride 2 Recovery.

Sierra Club Military Outdoors

www.sierraclub.org/military-outdoors

This group offers outings, club support events, social events, and activist events. Former service members with outdoor leadership training staff the programs.

Soul River Inc.

www.soulriverinc.org

A Black-led nonprofit providing healing outdoor experiences for veterans. It focuses on bringing veterans as mentors together with inner city youth and into the wild rivers of nature.

Team Red, White, and Blue (Team RWB)

www.teamrwb.org

This program offers exercise activities, local races, athletic events, social events, community service events, and leadership development.

Team River Runner

www.teamriverrunner.org

This organization provides all veterans and their families an opportunity to find health, healing, community purpose, and new challenges through adventure and adaptive paddle sports.

The Pam and George Wendt Foundation (formerly the OARS Foundation)

www.oars.com

This veteran adventure outfitter provides meaningful guided river rafting and outdoor adventure experiences.

Veteran Expeditions

www.vetexpeditions.com

This group offers backpacking trips, mountaineering expeditions, rock climbing, mountain biking, and golfing to veterans.

Warrior Bonfire Program

www.warriorbonfireprogram.org

A program that seeks to improve the lives of veterans through recreational and group therapies, memorial bonfire ceremonies, fishing, hunting, skiing, rafting, kayaking, surfing, hiking, and more.

Warrior Expeditions

https://warriorexpeditions.org

Warrior Hike, Warrior Bike, and Warrior Paddle help veterans transition from their wartime experiences through long-distance outdoor expeditions.

Warrior Institute for Rehabilitation and Optimal Conditioning

www.warriorinstitute.org

This institute uses outdoor recreation as a therapeutic medium to enhance the quality of life for military service members, veterans, and their families.

Warriors on Cataract Canyon

www.warriorsoncataract.org

A beneficial recreation program for VA hospitals to include in their treatment and recovery programs, Warriors on Cataract Canyon sponsors four-day whitewater trips on the Colorado River through Canyonlands National Park from Moab to Lake Powell for our disabled veterans. This trip gives the Wounded Warrior participants new hope and perspective and is an avenue toward forming a support group of other combat veterans, thereby putting them on a path to recovery and reintegration.

Wasatch Adaptive Sports

https://wasatchadaptivesports.org

The organization offers backcountry awareness clinics for veterans, summer retreats, introduction to mountain recreation clinics for veterans, and adaptive yoga. It targets veterans who are coping with military-related physical, cognitive, and emotional difficulties.

Wounded Warrior Project/Project Odyssey
www.woundedwarriorproject.org
This program gives veterans the tools to overcome the obstacles they face. It offers all-male, all-female, or couples retreats, that feature activities like hiking, rock climbing, scavenger hunts, and more. Multiday adventure with trained counselors and fellow warriors provide the opportunity to forge strong friendships and for self-discovery. The experiences gained from Project Odyssey help veterans work through challenges related to combat stress and improve their mental health and outlook.

National Suicide Prevention Lifeline
suicidepreventionlifeline.org
1-800-273-8255
The National Suicide Prevention Lifeline is a national network of local crisis centers that provides free and confidential emotional support to people in suicidal crisis or emotional distress 24 hours a day, 7 days a week. They are committed to improving crisis services and advancing suicide prevention by empowering individuals, advancing professional best practices, and building awareness.

BIBLIOGRAPHY

THE FOLLOWING MEDIA, STUDIES, AND other resources formed the basis of research as I met veterans and worked to share their stories.

ARTICLES

Applewhite, Larry, Derrick Arincorayan, and Barry Adams. "Exploring the prevalence of adverse childhood experiences in soldiers seeking behavioral health care during a combat deployment." *Military Medicine*, vol. 181,10 (2016): 1275–1280.

Atchley, Ruth Ann, David L. Strayer, and Paul Atchley. "Creativity in the Wild: Improving Creative Reasoning through Immersion in Natural Settings." *Public Library of Science.* December 2012.

Benac, Nancy. "The Long, Unfortunate History of Friendly Fire Accidents in U.S. Conflicts." *PBS News Hour.* June 11, 2014.

Bettmann, Joanna E., David E. Scheinfeld, Kort C. Prince, Eric L. Garland, and Katherine V. Ovrom. "Changes in Psychiatric Symptoms and Psychological Processes among Veterans Participating in a Therapeutic Adventure Program." *Psychological Services.* 2018.

Bratman, Gregory N., J. Paul Hamilton, Kevin S. Hahn, Gretchen C. Daily, and James J. Gross "Nature Reduces Rumination and Subgenal Prefrontal Cortex Activation "Nature reduces rumination and subgenal prefrontal cortex activation." ResearchGate.net. July 2015.

Cirino, Erica. "Why You Should Get (and Give) More Hugs." Healthline .com. April 2018.

Davis-Berman, Jennifer, Dene Berman, and Nathan D. Berman. "Outdoor Programs as Treatment for Post-traumatic Stress Disorder in Veterans: Issues and Evidence." *Best Practice in Mental Health An International Journal.* 2018.

DiGiuilio, Sarah. "Why Scientists Say Experiencing Awe Can Help You Live Your Best Life." NBCNews.com. February 2019.

Emmons, Robert. "How gratitude leads to a happier life." RobertEmmons.com. 2020.

Fetters, Ashley. "Where is the Black *Blueberries for Sal*?" The lack of diversity in children's books about nature." TheAtlantic.com. May 2019.

Frey, William, H., D. DeSota-Johnson, C. Hoffman, and J.T. McCall. "Effect of Stimulus on the Chemical Composition of Human Tears" *American Journal of Ophthalmology.* 1981.

Greer, Michael, and Neomi Vin-Raviv. "Outdoor-Based Therapeutic Recreation Programs among Military Veterans with Posttraumatic Stress Disorder: Accessing Evidence." *Military Behavioral Health.* 2019.

Hansen, Jennifer. "Crying Is a Sign of Strength, Not Weakness." Enlightened Solutions.com. October 2016.

Keller, Jared. "The Top 5 Reasons Soldiers Really Join the Army, According to Junior Enlisted" Task and Purpose.com. May 2018.

Markham, Heidi. "Why Hiking Is the Perfect Mind-Body Workout." Time.com. July 2017.

McDonald, Mary Catharine, Marisa Brandt, and Robyn Bluhm. "From Shell-Shock to PTSD, a Century of Invisible War Trauma." TheConversation.com. April 2017.

Mittal, Apoorva. "Leaving the Military Is Harder for Female Vets." *Military Times.* July 2019.

Morgan, Edward. "Big pharma and organized crime: They are more similar than you may think." Prepare for Change.com. April 2017.

Neighmond, Patricia. "Exercise Can Reduce Chronic Pain, Researchers Say." NPR.com. September 9, 2019.

Neuman, Scott. "Soldier Speaks up a Decade after Pat Tillman's Friendly Fire Death" NPR WVIA.com. April 2014.

O'Connor, Tom. "U.S. Special Forces Commander Says Soldiers 'Are Suffering' from over 15 Years of War." *Newsweek.* May 2017.

Poulsen, Dorthe Varning. "Nature-Based Therapy as a Treatment for Veterans with PTSD: What Do We Know?" *Journal of Public Mental Health*. 2017.

Reiner, Andrew. "The Power of Touch, Especially for Men." *New York Times*. December 2017.

Richtel, Matt. "The Latest in Military Strategy: Mindfulness." *New York Times*. April 2019.

Robinson, Lawrence, Melinda Smith, Jeanne Segal, and Jennifer Shubin. "Benefits of Play for Adults." Helpguide.org. December 2019.

Schlanger, Zoë. "Dirt Has a Microbiome, and It May Double as an Antidepressant" Quartz.com. May 2017.

Shane, Leo, III. "New Veteran Suicide Numbers Raise Concerns among Experts Hoping for Positive News" *Military Times*. October 2019.

Siler, Wes. "For Veterans, Outdoor Therapy Could Become Law." Outside .com. May 2019.

Sneed, R.S. and S. Cohen. "A Prospective Study of Volunteerism and Hypertension Risk in Older Adults." *Psychology and Aging,* 28(2), 578–586.

Steele, Erik. "How the 19-Year-Old Brain Can Both Awe and Appall Us." BangorDailynews.com. April 2013.

Sukel, Kayt. December. "How Military Service Changes the Brain." *Neuroscience Dana Foundation.* 2017.

Suttie, Jill. "How Nature Boosts Kindness, Happiness, Creativity." Mindful .com. March 2016.

Townsend., Jasmine, Brent L. Hawkins, Jessie L. Bennett, Jamie Hoffman, Tamar Martin, Elaine Sotherden, and William Bridges. "Preliminary Long-Term Health Outcomes Associated with Recreation-Based Health and Wellness Programs for Injured Service Members." *Cogent Psychology.* 2018.

Tull, Matthew, PhD. "How to Practice Being Mindful" Verywellmind.com. June 2019.

US Department of Veterans Affairs, "2019 National Suicide Prevention Annual Report, from the Office of Mental Health and Suicide Prevention." 2019.

FILMS

Beresford-Kroeger, Diana. *Call of the Forest: The Forgotten Wisdom of Trees.*
2016.

BOOKS

Amos, M. Clifford. *Your Guide to Forest Bathing: Experience the Healing Power of Nature.* Newburyport, MA: Red Wheel Publishing, 2018.

Bromet, Evelyn J., Elie G. Karam, Karestan C. Koenen, and Dan J. Stein, eds. *Trauma and Post-traumatic Stress Disorder: Global Perspectives from the WHO World Mental Health Surveys.* Boston: Cambridge University Press, 2018.

Couch, Dick. *Sua Sponte: The Forging of a Modern American Ranger.* New York: Penguin, 2013.

DeBenedet, M.D., Anthony T. *Playful Intelligence: The Power of Living Lightly in a Serious World.* Santa Monica, CA: Santa Monica Press, 2018.

Donaldson, David, and Maurice J. Forrester. *A Grip on the Mane of Life: An Authorized Biography of Earl V. Shaffer.* Gardners: Appalachian Trail Museum, 2015.

Dungy, Camille. *Black Nature: Four Centuries of African American Nature Poetry.* Athens: University of Georgia Press, 2009.

Dustin, Daniel L , Kelly Bricker, Sandra Negley, Matthew Brownlee, Keri Schwab, and Neil Lundberg, eds. *Nature's Grace: America's Veterans and the Healing Power of Nature.* Urbana, IL: Sagamore Publishing, 2018.

Dustin, Daniel, Kelly Bricker, Matthew Brownlee, Keri Schwab, and Neil Lundberg. *This Land is Your Land: Toward a Better Understanding of Nature's Resiliency-Building and Restorative Power for Armed Forces Personnel, Veterans, and Their Families.* Urbana: Sagamore Publishing, 2016.

Jung, Carl. *Letters, Volume 1.* Princeton, NJ: Princeton University Press, 1973.

———. *The Collected Works of CG Jung, Volume 18: The Symbolic Life.* Princeton, NJ: Princeton University Press, 1977.

Falke, Ken, and Josh Goldberg. *Struggle Well: Thriving in the Aftermath of Trauma.* Austin, TX: Lioncrest Publishing, 2018.

Grossman, Dave. *On Killing: The Psychological Cost of Learning to Kill in War and Society.* New York: Back Bay Books, 2009.

Merzenich, Michael. *Soft-Wired: How the New Science of Brain Plasticity Can Change Your Life, 2nd ed.* San Francisco: Parnassus Publishing, 2013.

Norman, Michael. *These Good Men.* New York: Random House, 1991.

Palmer, Parker J. *Let Your Life Speak: Listening for the Voice of Vocation.* San Francisco: Jossey Bass, 1999.

Peacock, Doug. *Walking it Off: A Veteran's Chronicle of War and Wilderness.* Cheney, WA: Eastern Washington University Press, 2005.

Resick, Patricia A., Candace M. Monson, and Kathleen M. Chard. *Cognitive Processing Therapy for PTSD: A Comprehensive Manual.* New York: The Guilford Press, 2016.

Ross, Cindy. *Journey on the Crest: Walking 2600 Miles from Canada to Mexico.* Seattle: Mountaineers Books, 1987.

Shaffer, Earl V. *Walking with Spring.* Harper's Ferry: Appalachian Trail Conservancy, 1983.

ADDITIONAL SUGGESTED READING

Capps, Ron. *Writing War: A Guide to Telling Your Own Story.* Silver Spring, MD: The Veterans Writing Project, 2014.

Carpenter, Kyle, and Don Yeager. *You Are Worth It: Building a Life Worth Fighting For.* New York: William Morrow, 2019.

Covington, P. W. *Vet to Vet: An Examination of PTSD Through Writing.* London: Hercules Publishing, 2011

Fanning, Rory. *Worth Fighting For: An Army Ranger's Journey Out of the Military and Across America.* Chicago: Haymarket Books, 2014.

Finkel, David. *The Good Soldiers.* New York: Picador, Farrar, Straus, and Giroux, 2009.

———. *Thank You for Your Service.* New York: Picador, Farrar, Straus, and Giroux, 2013.

Gambone, Michael D. *Long Journeys Home American Veterans of World War II, Korea, and Vietnam (Volume 156).* College Station: Texas A & M University Press, 2017.

Guerin, Dava, and Kevin Ferris. *Vets and Pets: Wounded Warriors and the Animals that Help Heal Them.* New York: Skyhorse Publishing, 2017.

Hoge, Charles W. *Once a Warrior—Always a Warrior: Navigating The Transition From Combat To Home—Including Combat Stress, PTSD, and MTBI.* Guilford: Lyons Press, 2010.

Junger, Sebastian. *Tribe: On Homecoming and Belonging.* Twelve New York: Hachette Book Group, 2016.

——. *WAR.* Twelve New York: Hachette Book Group, 2010.

Klay, Phil. *Redeployment.* New York: Penguin Books, 2014.

O'Brien, Tim. *The Things They Carried.* Boston: Mariner Books/Houghton Mifflin, 1990.

Powers, Kevin. *The Yellow Birds.* New York: Back Bay Books, 2013.

Roszak, Theodore, Mary E. Gomes, and Allen D. Kanner, eds. *Ecopsychology: Restoring the Earth, Healing the Mind.* San Francisco: Sierra Club Books, 1995.

Sherman, Nancy. *The Untold War: Inside the Hearts, Minds, and Souls of Our Soldiers.* New York: W. W. Norton, 2010.

Van der Kolk, M.D, Bessel. *The Body Keeps the Score: Brain, Mind and Body in the Healing of Trauma.* New York: Viking, 2014.

Westlund, Stephanie. *Field Exercises: How Veterans are Healing Themselves through Farming and Other Outdoor Activities.* Gabriola Island, BC: New Society Publishers, 2014.

Wood, David. *What Have We Done: The Moral Injury of Our Longest Wars.* New York: Little, Brown, 2016.

ABOUT THE AUTHOR

CINDY ROSS HAS LED A life of adventure, embracing the joys and therapeutic powers of the natural world. A long-distance hiker with the Triple Crown to her credit, she directs the non-profit River House PA for veterans. She writes about healing through nature for a variety of publications, including *Stars & Stripes, Military Times, Yoga Journal,* and *Appalachian Trail Journeys.* Cindy is the author of eight books, including *Scraping Heaven: A Family's Journey Along the Continental Divide, The World Is Our Classroom: How One Family Used Nature and Travel to Shape an Extraordinary Education,* and most recently, *The Log Cabin Years: How One Couple Built a Home from Scratch and Created a Life.* She lives with her husband, Todd Gladfelter, in New Ringgold, Pennsylvania, near the Appalachian Trail.

ABOUT THE ILLUSTRATOR

BRYCE GLADFELTER IS A NOMADIC illustrator and rapper, who honed his skills in the arts while traveling the world and adventuring in the outdoors. His work aims to provide a window into the human spirit. The newly released children's book *No Reading Allowed* showcases his eclectic range of style.

MOUNTAINEERS BOOKS is a leading publisher of mountaineering literature and guides—including our flagship title, *Mountaineering: The Freedom of the Hills*—as well as adventure narratives, natural history, and general outdoor recreation. Through our two imprints, Skipstone and Braided River, we also publish titles on sustainability and conservation. We are committed to supporting the environmental and educational goals of our organization by providing expert information on human-powered adventure, sustainable practices at home and on the trail, and preservation of wilderness.

The Mountaineers, founded in 1906, is a 501(c)(3) nonprofit outdoor recreation and conservation organization whose mission is to enrich lives and communities by helping people "explore, conserve, learn about, and enjoy the lands and waters of the Pacific Northwest and beyond." One of the largest such organizations in the United States, it sponsors classes and year-round outdoor activities throughout the Pacific Northwest, including climbing, hiking, backcountry skiing, snowshoeing, camping, kayaking, sailing, and more. The Mountaineers also supports its mission through its publishing division, Mountaineers Books, and promotes environmental education and citizen engagement. For more information, visit The Mountaineers Program Center, 7700 Sand Point Way NE, Seattle, WA 98115-3996; phone 206-521-6001; www.mountaineers.org; or email info@mountaineers.org.

Our publications are made possible through the generosity of donors and through sales of 700 titles on outdoor recreation, sustainable lifestyle, and conservation. To donate, purchase books, or learn more, visit us online:

MOUNTAINEERS BOOKS
1001 SW Klickitat Way, Suite 201 • Seattle, WA 98134
800-553-4453 • mbooks@mountaineersbooks.org • www.mountaineersbooks.org

An independent nonprofit publisher since 1960

OTHER TITLES YOU MIGHT ENJOY FROM MOUNTAINEERS BOOKS

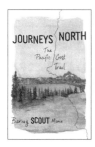

JOURNEYS NORTH
The Pacific Crest Trail
Barney Scout Mann
"[T]he next best thing to being on the Pacific Crest Trail yourself!" —Richard Louv

JOURNEY ON THE CREST
Walking 2600 Miles from Mexico to Canada
Cindy Ross
"Ross writes with an ear for dialogue and an eye for detail."—*Publishers Weekly*

SCRAPING HEAVEN
A Family's Journey Along the Continental Divide
Cindy Ross
"Well written, captivating and incredibly educational, this adventure is a lesson in life's simplicity and the beauty of accomplishment." —*Publishers Weekly*

MUD, ROCKS, BLAZES
Letting Go on the Appalachian Trail
Heather "Anish" Anderson
"Beautiful and deftly written and intimate and searing in its honesty." —*Foreword Reviews*

WAY OUT THERE
Adventures of a Wilderness Trekker
J. R. Harris
Engaging tales of nearly fifty years of wanderlust and adventure.